Lord, Teach Me To Pray
in 28 Days

Kay Arthur

HARVEST HOUSE PUBLISHERS
EUGENE, OREGON

Cover by Koechel Peterson & Associates, Inc., Minneapolis, Minnesota

Cover photo © Monique Rodriguez

LORD, TEACH ME TO PRAY IN 28 DAYS
Revised and updated
Copyright © 1982/2008 by Kay Arthur
Published by Harvest House Publishers
Eugene, Oregon 97408
www.harvesthousepublishers.com

Library of Congress Cataloging-in-Publication Data

Arthur, Kay, 1933-
Lord, teach me to pray in 28 days / Kay Arthur.
  p. cm.
ISBN 978-0-7369-2360-6 (pbk.)
ISBN 978-0-7369-3270-7 (eBook)
1. Prayer—Christianity. I. Title.
BV215.A77 2008
248.3'2—dc22

                                                              2008023046

Printed in the United States of America

23 24 25 26 / BP-NI / 27 26 25 24 23 22

CONTENTS

WEEK FOUR: Staying in the Word

As You Begin...

Are you hurting, Beloved?
Does the pain run deep?
And when I call you "Beloved," do you believe it?

Do you ever find yourself wondering whether you are truly loved by anyone—even God? Then again, perhaps pain isn't the issue in your life right now. Even so, you feel torn by confusion, stress, or doubts. Perhaps you're so pressured, so burdened, and so weighed down that you wonder how you're going to make it.

The news is bad

> *the situation difficult*

>> *the crisis overwhelming*

>>> *the insecurity debilitating*

>>>> *the decision-making process scary.*

On any given day you can find yourself concerned about any or all of the following: yourself, your spouse (having one, not having one), children (wishing, wanting, having, wishing you didn't), your friends, your finances. The future. The past. The present.

What will you do? How will you make it? Where will you turn?

There are answers to those questions, loved one, and you can find them in the Word of God and in prayer, as you cast all your cares on Him because He cares for you.

The Word of God is the foundation for everything else in our lives. According to Jesus Himself, man lives by every word that comes out of the mouth of God. The Word of God is God-breathed. That's the very term the apostle Paul used in his letter to young Timothy:

All Scripture is inspired by God and profitable for teaching, for reproof, for correction, for training in righteousness; so that the man of God may be adequate, equipped for every good work (2 Timothy 3:16).

The word "inspired" in this passage comes from a Greek word that literally means "God-breathed." When God speaks on any given issue, what He speaks is truth. What He commands is to be obeyed. God has spoken and it stands. We are to believe and obey.

Yet being a Christian is more than merely believing promises and obeying commands. At its very essence, Christianity isn't a religion, it's a *relationship*. And as we all know, a relationship requires a high commitment to communication.

That's where prayer comes in. It is through prayer that you and I communicate with our heavenly Father.

Think about the everyday needs and demands in our lives: the decisions we must make, the wisdom we need, the resources we require, the relationships that need so much tending, discernment, and sacrifice. Is it any wonder the Bible says, "Pray without ceasing"?

We need the strength, wisdom, and love of the Lord in our lives, and we need these things desperately.

Though Scripture sets forth all of the goals and standards for everyday life in principle, it usually doesn't fill in the practical details. That's why we need to talk and listen to our heavenly Father.

This, Beloved, is prayer. And that's what this study is all about—learning to pray God's way, according to His Word. It's about learning how to talk to God anytime about anything and everything. Or to put it in words that resonate with our spirit, prayer is about communion with God.

This journey of learning you're about to embark on has already been completed by hundreds of thousands of people all over the world, many of whom have written to Precept Ministries with testimonies of what a help and an encouragement it has been in their lives.

I offer this book with the prayer that God will use it mightily to teach you to pray "according to His will," and that His words on prayer will abide in you. Remember, Jesus said, "If you abide in Me, and My words abide in you, ask whatever you wish, and it will be done for you" (John 15:7).

I am so excited about the truths you are going to learn from the precious Word of God in the following pages, and the incredible difference I *know* they will make in your life and in your relationship with the sovereign ruler of the universe. In just four short weeks we will learn God's basic precepts on prayer—principles that will give you a thoroughgoing biblical understanding of this crucial area of life.

What you learn in this study, dear child of God, will be yours to put into practice for a lifetime, just as Jesus intended when He taught His own disciples how to pray.

Learning to Pray God's Way

Faith Is a Relationship

When the apostles of the early church suddenly found themselves embroiled in a controversy that consumed both their time and energy, they had enough spiritual presence of mind to know something *had* to be done. This was a very serious situation for the infant church. The apostles were in danger of missing the priority of their highest callings—the Word of God and prayer.

As a result, they summoned "the congregation of the disciples and said, 'It is not desirable for us to neglect the word of God in order to serve tables. Therefore, brethren, select from among you seven men of good reputation, full of the Spirit and of wisdom, whom we may put in charge of this task. But we will devote ourselves to prayer and to the ministry of the word'" (Acts 6:2-4).

What wisdom! The apostles had to be careful lest they become so occupied with *serving* God that they neglected the Word, which is *knowing* God, and prayer, which is *communicating* with Him. Serving God, valuable as that might be, is no substitute for knowing Him and communicating with Him. Real service flows out of relationship, not obligation.

A healthy, strong, and vital relationship is based on communication: speaking, listening, and understanding. This is why, when the pressures of leadership over the affairs of the early church became too much, these leaders knew they had to take immediate steps to change their situation. And that's just what they did, taking action that gave rise to the very first church deacons.

Seeing what they did will help us too, so take a moment and open your Bible to Acts 6. In this study I'll be asking you to read from your own Bible, so you can mark it and note exactly what God is teaching you in that passage. (If you will actually do this you will find it will make an incredible difference in your study. Many—thousands—of men and women could happily confirm this.)

> **Read the first four verses of Acts 6 and list two things to which these early church leaders determined to devote themselves.**
>
> 1. _____
>
> 2. _____
>
> **You might want to mark these words in your Bible. It would be good to choose a color, symbol, or both for each and then color-code your Bible as you do this study. Personally, I mark *Word* by drawing a symbol of an open book like this with a fine-point purple pen (purple is the color of royalty) and coloring it green. Green is my color for life, growth. I mark prayer like this. It symbolizes to me the cupping of two hands raised in prayer. I color it pink. You do what fits you! If marking is a new thing, just let me say that once you break down and do it, you will see it works! It's tremendously effective—and has in a sense become a science!**

Now then, let's pause for a moment and reflect on our priorities as well. It was the very busyness of life, the pressures of ministry, that caused the Twelve to stop and reflect on what was most important. But busyness didn't stop after the first century, did it? Too often we find ourselves in a dizzying whirlwind of activities, responsibilities, and ministries to others. In the midst of our busy lives and multiple ministries to others, we need to periodically stop and evaluate our priorities. Otherwise we too might very well neglect the essentials.

> **What are your top two priorities for every day? What are your *"these-are-what-I-am-determined-***

to-do-day-in-and-day-out" hopes? Be honest in your answer, for God meets us in our objective honesty. Writing out your priorities is helpful as well.

1. _____

2. _____

The apostles knew that prayer and the ministry of the Word were absolutely vital. They were building the church, and the church had to be built on the solid foundation of truth. To neglect the Word of God would be nothing short of disaster.

Do you understand what they meant when they spoke of the "ministry of the word" in Acts 6:4?

Jesus gave a clear definition of "the word" on His way to the garden of Gethsemane, where He was betrayed and arrested. Let's see what Jesus prayed on behalf of the disciples and all who would believe in Him…which, Beloved, includes you! (By the way, *Beloved* was a term used by the writers of the New Testament epistles—men writing to men and women. I wanted you to know that so you men don't cringe. Just being biblical!)

> In His time of crisis, what did Jesus desire for you and me? You can find the answer in John 17:17.
>
> (Of course, I'd like for you to read more of Jesus' prayer to His Father, in verses 1-17, so you can see the context—so vital in handling the Word of God accurately—but if you're in a rush, I understand.)

_____

_____

_____

_____

Read verse 17 in your Bible, and record what the verse says.

_____

_____

Someone has said that prayer and the Word are like two wings of a bird—both are necessary if the bird is to fly. And both are necessary for us if we want to soar in our relationship with our heavenly Father. As did the apostles, we must give ourselves first and foremost to prayer and to the ministry of the Word. These twin priorities make a dramatic difference in the vitality of your relationship with God.

As you discovered in John 17:17, God's Word sanctifies us, setting us apart from the world for Him. Never forget that God's Word—from the first verse of Genesis to the last verse in Revelation—is pure truth! You can trust it completely, dear one.

Let's look at another verse that shows us the interlocking of prayer and the Word. Read John 15:7 in your Bible, and in one simple sentence write what you observed from this verse about the relationship of the Word and prayer.

_____

_____

_____

_____

By the way, if you were to mark all references to prayer in your Bible, what synonym for prayer would you mark in this verse?

_____

Finally, let's look at 1 John 5:13-15. Because these verses contain such precious promises, the passage is printed for you so you won't miss a one.

Read these verses aloud, underlining or highlighting every use of "you," "we," and "us." Color-code them. (I always color-code the recipients in an epistle orange, and the author blue.) Then read the passage a second time and mark every reference to prayer. While you won't find the specific word *pray*, there is a synonym.

> 13 *These things I have written to you who believe in the name of the Son of God, so that you may know that you have eternal life.*
> 14 *This is the confidence which we have before Him, that, if we ask anything according to His will, He hears us.*
> 15 *And if we know that He hears us in whatever we ask, we know that we have the requests which we have asked from Him.*

Now look at every place you underlined "you," "we," and "us," and list every truth you learned from marking the text this way.

_____

_____

_____

_____

_____

What did you learn about prayer, or *asking*, from these verses? The answer is right there in the text. Just look where you marked the word "ask," and write down what you observe.

_____

_____

_____

Now, reason with me: If you want God to hear you and provide what you ask, then you need to ask according to His will. And how will you know His will, Beloved? By listening to—knowing—His Word!

God speaks in His Word, and we are to listen; we speak in prayer and God listens. Awesome! Doesn't this truth make you want to give yourself to prayer and to the Word?

It's Time to Pray

This daily feature provides you with a wonderful opportunity to hear from God, speak to Him in prayer, record your thoughts, and record how He speaks to you. If you're like me, you'll find yourself wanting more time with Him each passing day.

So what is your prayer today in light of what you've learned? Make it short and simple. Write it here, and look back later to see how He specifically answers your specific requests. What a faith-builder that will be in your life!

*Oh, God, I...*_____

_____

_____

Prayer Keeps Us Connected

As we discovered together yesterday, Christianity is a relationship, and good communication is essential to all such relationships. In any relationship it is essential to listen, hear, and understand one another. Communication begins with God. He is the initiator of our salvation, and He does that by getting the good news of the gospel to us through His Word and through His people.

THE GOOD NEWS OF GOD

The apostle Paul defines the gospel, or good news, in 1 Corinthians 15:1-8. Stop and read this passage in your Bible now. Briefly condensed, the good news according to the Scriptures is:

Jesus died for our sins and was buried (verses 3-4).

He rose again on the third day and was seen by many (verses 4-8).

Let's think about this good news for a few minutes. God sent His Son—His only begotten Son, born of a virgin (and therefore without the sin that every human has at birth)—to die for our sins. Your sins, and mine.

When Jesus was crucified, God took those sins of ours—the sins of the whole world—and placed them on Jesus so He might become sin for us, giving us His very righteousness in exchange (2 Corinthians 5:21).

Stand in wonder, Beloved, at the love that would cause the one and only true God to give His sinless Son so you and I might have eternal life. "God demonstrates His own love toward us, in that while we were yet sinners, Christ died for us" (Romans 5:8).

What is the proof of eternal life? It is the second point of the gospel: God raised Jesus Christ from the dead, never to die again. The wages or payment for sin is death (Romans 6:23). Because a sinless Jesus satisfied God's holiness and paid our debt in full, those who believe in Jesus pass from death to life.

If we are true children of God, death will be like falling asleep on earth and waking up in the presence of God Almighty. You'll exhale your last breath of earthly air and in the next moment, draw new lungs full of celestial air. For the believer, death is coming home! Living in His presence forever and ever! Never to die a second death, which is the lake of fire (Revelation 20:6,14)! Oh, it is time to talk to God, Beloved (are you realizing you can talk to Him anytime?) and to say, "Hallelujah! Praise be to You for so great a salvation."

Do you have forgiveness of sins? Do you have Jesus? They go together! Do you believe He is the Son of God, the only Savior? Have you received Him as your Savior, your Lord, your God?

Look at John 1:12. What is God's promise?

_____

_____

Are you God's child? How do you know? What is the proof of your salvation?

_____

_____

_____

_____

If you're not sure, then ask God during this study—even today—to bring you into His forever family. And when He does, may I suggest you write down the date? I was saved at age 29 on July 16, 1963, when

I moved from a religion to a relationship. (I know—you're doing the math to figure out my age!) My changed life (I was a mess) is the evidence of my salvation (2 Corinthians 5:17). But I love knowing the date when I was born again (John 3:1-18). It is the most important day of my life. It's when I truly began to live!

Now then, look at one more thing in 1 Corinthians 15:1-2. When we hear, receive, and stand in this glorious gospel, we are saved—rescued from a meaningless life, rescued from death, rescued from hell. And we hold fast to that salvation. Endurance is evidence of your salvation. May I suggest you read these verses in your Bible and underline the verbs you just read: *received, stand, saved, hold fast*. (If you have a different translation, look for words with these meanings.) Standing firm is a valuable truth that you don't want to pass over lightly.

GOD'S WORD IS TRUTH

When God communicates with humanity, we hear truth—and we either accept it or reject it. But what we or anyone else thinks about the Bible doesn't change what it is at its essence: the very words of God Himself. According to 2 Timothy 3:16 and 2 Peter 1:21, God's Word was inspired, or "God-breathed" (the Greek word is *theopneustos*) through human scribes, so that holy men of God spoke and wrote as they were inspired by the Spirit of God. According to the Bible itself, the Bible is God's Word and it is truth, God's communication to humankind.

Let's review. What, then, is prayer?

Prayer is... _____

_____

_____

_____

What role is prayer to take in our lives? How important should it be? How important is prayer to you at this time in your life?

_____

_____

_____

_____

_____

How Often Are We to Pray?

Look up 1 Thessalonians 5:17 in your Bible, and answer that question from the Word of God. (Don't forget to mark prayer in your Bible.)

I am to pray... _____

_____

_____

What does this really mean? That I'm to stay on my knees in a specific place doing nothing but praying? For heaven's sake, no! Note I said, "for heaven's sake." We must be about our Father's business, and that requires us getting into the world and not only offering others the Word of truth, but also showing them by our lives how life is to be lived out in circumstances just like theirs!

What does it mean, then, to "pray without ceasing"? It means to stay in communication with God, to talk to your Father about everything. I see it as a command to walk in continual dependence upon Him, realizing that He is a God who is there. He is a God who will supply all my needs, from the need to worship to the need for protection from the evil one. In other words, I am to commune with Him nonstop as if He were by my side at all times—which He is! When we live like this, we show our dependence on Him and the value we place on His wisdom and leadership in our lives.

With every day that goes by, I see more and more people wearing those little cell phones clipped to one ear. I'm sure you've noticed. It used to look so strange and unusual, but the practice is becoming more common all the time. You see these users of mini cell phones seemingly talking into empty space, and when they look your way, it's as if they're looking right through you. Walking around with a phone clipped to your ear, however, doesn't mean you're always talking. But it *does* mean you can be connected at a moment's notice—wherever you are, whatever you're doing.

When you see those ear-clip cell phones, let them remind you to stay connected with God—to not only talk to Him about everything but also tell Him throughout the day how much you love Him, need Him, appreciate Him, and depend on Him. To pray without ceasing is to stay connected!

FOLLOWING JESUS' EXAMPLE

When Jesus was with the disciples on earth, He was our living example of how God intended for us to live. What Adam failed to do and be in the Garden of Eden, Jesus—the Last Adam (Romans 5:14; 1 Corinthians 15:45)—accomplished perfectly.

Those who became Jesus' disciples not only heard His teaching on the importance of prayer, they also observed it in His life. After Jesus prayed in a certain place, one of His disciples said to Him, *"Lord, teach us to pray"* (Luke 11:1).

Oh, what precious words those are to me! Can you guess why? Because they show me that *prayer is a skill that can be learned.* If prayer is a skill, then it is something I can develop with time and practice. And that gives me great hope!

Sometimes I think we allow ourselves to become intimidated when we hear of the faith and prayer life of others. We say to ourselves, *I could never attain that.* As a result, we become defeated before we ever begin. We read of saints who spent multiple hours—or entire days and nights—on their knees in prayer, and we can't seem to pray more than ten minutes at a stretch. How then could we ever pray for hours each day, let alone whole days or nights? Feeling like we could never do such a thing, we give up before we ever begin.

But that's not true. You *can* develop and maintain a life-giving, ongoing conversation with your Creator. Just know that it will only come little by little with knowledge, application, time, and experience. The disciples knew this, and so they began where each of us must begin if we are ever to learn.

They began with a hunger to be taught.

They had seen Jesus praying, and they knew *He* understood how to pray if anybody did! So they took their hunger for a deeper experience of prayer to *the* Expert. And that is where you and I will be going in this study: to the Expert, the Lord Jesus Christ, the Word of God.

In the context of Luke 11, Jesus answered the disciples' request by giving them what we call "the Lord's Prayer." Take a moment and read Luke 11:1-4 in your Bible. You might want to mark the references to prayer in your Bible as you read it.

When He gave them this prayer, did Jesus mean they were to simply pray this prayer over and over? The answer is seen in comparing Scripture with Scripture.

Read Matthew 6:6-13, which is printed out below.
As you read it, mark or color code every reference
to praying in the text.

> 6 *"When you pray, go into your inner room,*
> *close your door and pray to your Father*

who is in secret, and your Father who sees
what is done in secret will reward you.

7 "And when you are praying, do not use
meaningless repetition as the Gentiles do,
for they suppose that they will be heard for
their many words.

8 "So do not be like them; for your Father
knows what you need before you ask Him.

9 "Pray, then, in this way:
'Our Father who is in heaven, hallowed be
Your name.

10 'Your kingdom come. Your will be done, on
earth as it is in heaven.

11 'Give us this day our daily bread.

12 'And forgive us our debts, as we also have
forgiven our debtors.

13 'And do not lead us into temptation, but
deliver us from evil. [For Yours is the kingdom and the power and the glory forever.
Amen.]'"

Now, what do you learn from marking the references to praying? List your observations below.

_____

_____

_____

_____

_____

_____

The Lord's Prayer is a way to pray, isn't it? Jesus said, "Pray, then, *in this way.*" In other words, "pray like this," or, "pray according to this method."

The Lord never intended this prayer to be repeated over and over by rote, like some kind of religious duty or magic formula. No, Jesus was using the same manner of instruction that the rabbis of the day used. He was teaching the disciples an *index* for prayer.

Index prayers were a collection of brief sentences, each of which suggested a subject for prayer. *I believe, as do others, that the Lord's Prayer states for us in topical form all the ingredients necessary for effective prayer.*

Nowhere else is it recorded in God's Word that the disciples said to Jesus, "Teach us to pray. " Nowhere else did Jesus directly say, "Pray, then, *in this way*" (Matthew 6:9). The conclusion couldn't be more clear: To pray according to the index or the outline of the Lord's Prayer is to pray with effectiveness and power.

Why don't you covenant before God that without fail you will set aside a specific time for prayer each day through the course of this study? Tell Him that you come to Him as a learner, that if He doesn't help you there is no hope! During your prayer time, talk with Him about what you have learned. Don't compare yourself with others or try to measure up to their prayer lives. It's just you and God, child and Father.

He's waiting and eager to have that time alone with you.

> Look up the following verses in your Bible and again mark the references to prayer. Then list what you learned. When you observe a verse, use the old journalistic formula of asking the 5 W's and an H: *who, what, when, where, why,* and *how.* In these verses you are looking for the WHO (Jesus), WHAT He prayed about or what happened when He prayed, WHEN He prayed, WHERE He prayed, WHY He prayed, and HOW He prayed.

Luke 3:21-22 _____

_____

_____

Luke 5:16 _____

_____

_____

Luke 6:12-13 _____

_____

_____

Luke 11:1 _____

_____

_____

All of these questions won't necessarily be answered, but you don't want to miss the ones that are! Get in the practice, Beloved, of carefully observing the text when you study it. Never add to the Scriptures—even in your imagination—lest you stray from Truth or cause others to stray. God tells us everything He wants us to know, and we have plenty to learn without adding to His word. Keep silent when God is silent!

"Lord, teach us to pray..."

If you and I had been there, we would have asked for the same thing, wouldn't we? Jesus' disciples needed to know, and so do we. So here it is: a study of Jesus' response to His disciples when they said, "Lord, teach us to pray," and He replied, "When you pray, say..."

It's Time to Pray

Dear one, if you received Jesus today, then thank Him for the gift of eternal life. Share that decision with someone who can help you grow in Christ. Just think, now you belong to God's forever family. You may want to record the date of your decision here:

_____

Always Go to the Expert

Now then, my friend, before we go any further, may I ask you: What are your current feelings about your prayer life, your communication with God?

> Sometimes it helps to jot down words that describe where you are when it comes to prayer. What are your frustrations? Doubts? Desires? Fears? Are you just learning to approach God in prayer? Spill it all out to God. It's good to put your frustrations, hopes, and fears into words.

_____

_____

_____

_____

_____

_____

_____

You have probably often heard, "The effective prayer of a righteous man can accomplish much" (James 5:16). Yet what do those words really mean?

It's easy to feel inadequate when we read of giants of the faith like the prophet Elijah. Imagine praying and having the very heavens turn off the spigot for three years and six months—and then praying again and watching the sky pour rain and the earth produce its fruit! (See James 5:17-18.) Whew!

We tell ourselves, "Never, never, never could I ever pray like that! No, not me. Not an ordinary Christian like me. Praying and getting answers like that is for some 'supersaint.'"

Is it? Was that God's intention in having James record these words? Are they meant to be words of encouragement or intimidating words of defeat? Oh, Beloved, I know they are meant to be words of hope and encouragement! What God wants us to see is that regular, everyday people—like you and me—can accomplish extraordinary things through prayer.

You see, you *can* develop a meaningful prayer life! And you are beginning in the right place by committing yourself to this study. God knows your heart's desire, and He wants you to learn how to pray more than you do!

As you have already seen, the Lord's Prayer as recorded in Luke 11 is recorded in even greater detail in the Gospel of Matthew. Take a moment and read Matthew 6:5-13 in your own Bible. I am going to take you back further than I did yesterday. It will put you into context—the setting in which Jesus introduced "the way to pray."

It is so important for you to read Scripture in *context*. God doesn't speak in isolated, unrelated phrases. We don't speak that way either, most of the time—unless we are a frustrated parent! For this reason, you need to always check out the context, or the setting, whenever you study a portion of God's Word. As you do, remember: Context rules over all interpretation.

As you read Matthew 6:5-13, mark every reference to prayer. (If you don't want to mark your Bible right now with ink, feel free to use a pencil. Just remember there's nothing wrong with marking or writing in your Bible. The Bible is your textbook for life. God wants you to study and know it, and marking the text helps you do that.)

Now, let's do some observation. Let's see what the Word of God says in Matthew 6:5-13 about praying.

List below what you learn simply from marking the references to *praying*—and nothing more. Number your insights.

_____

_____

_____

As you read, you came across the word *hypocrites* (verse 5). A *hypocrite* is like a person who wears a mask. He is two-faced, saying one thing but meaning another. A hypocrite pretends to be something other than what he or she is!

As you saw yesterday, when Jesus gave the disciples this prayer, it was obvious from the context He was not giving them a prayer to pray, a prayer said as a mechanical repetition. That is what I did Sunday after Sunday for 29 years. I recited the words in a meaningless way. But then, wow! After I got saved, the words exploded with new meaning for me. What I was saying and what I was asking for were awesome, relevant, and weighty!

Then the day came when I discovered something else about the Lord's Prayer. I realized when Jesus said, "Pray in this way," He was giving the disciples a *way* to pray, not a prayer to pray. (Not that it's wrong to pray the Lord's Prayer!) As we have already noted, Jesus was employing the same manner of instruction that the rabbis (teachers) of His time used. He was teaching the disciples an index of the various topics to be covered in prayer.

As I mentioned, index prayers were a collection of brief sentences, each of which suggested a subject for prayer. Remember, books in biblical times were not plentiful for the average person. They were all copied by hand. The printing press didn't truly come into use until the 1400s! So teachers used learning devices or techniques such as index sentences. Memorizing the index sentence would prompt what someone was to remember or do.

The Ingredients of Effective Prayer

Let's take a look now at what is called the Lord's Prayer and determine the topic of each index sentence. Your assignment is to 1) pray, asking God to help you hear and understand what He is teaching in these verses—the issue of each sentence that you are to cover in prayer; and 2) write next to each sentence the topic or issue with which it deals.

Keep your answer as short as possible—one or two words, if you can. This is for you to think through, Beloved. It is so important to think. When you became God's child, He gave you the mind of Christ (1 Corinthians 2:16). Use it! Don't worry about being clever or eloquent in your titles. Don't think you have to use alliteration, making all the titles begin with the same letter. That's not the point. By now you know there is nothing eloquent about *my* writing or speech (if you've heard me on radio, television, or in person), yet God has been pleased to use me anyway. So relax. Let the Holy Spirit be your teacher and give you insight.

I have numbered the sentences in Matthew 6:9-13 for you. You can record the theme of each on the line next to it.

The Sentence	The Topic
1. Our Father who is in heaven, hallowed be Your name.	_____
2. Your kingdom come.	_____
3. Your will be done, on earth as it is in heaven.	_____
4. Give us this day our daily bread.	_____
5. And forgive us our debts, as we also have forgiven our debtors.	_____

6. And do not lead us into temptation, but deliver us from evil.

_____

7. For Yours is the kingdom and the power and the glory forever. Amen.

_____

Great! You have prayerfully thought this through, and I'm proud of you. We'll talk more about your answers tomorrow. Just know that my heart is so filled with gratitude and love for you. I am so proud of you for studying God's Word.

It's Time to Pray

Follow the example of your Lord and Savior, beloved child of God. Get alone with the Father and know that He is waiting and eager to have time alone with you.

Talk to your Father about one of the topics in the Lord's Prayer that has touched you where you are right now. Maybe you need deliverance from temptation, or forgiveness in a relationship, or to lay some specific need before Him. Or maybe you just want to worship Him. Whatever, take time to get alone and pray, "and your Father who sees what is done in secret will reward you" (Matthew 6:6). Write what is on your heart. Talk with Him about what you have learned.

_____

_____

_____

_____

_____

Come to the Father

Wouldn't it be wonderful if every single principle of prayer could be condensed into several simple sentences so you could remember them easily? Then no matter where you found yourself, you could recall those principles and use them to commune with your Father in a meaningful and vital way.

There is nothing, absolutely *nothing* sweeter than knowing you have touched the hem of His garment in prayer. It's healing and renewing. It brings a quietness and a confidence that flow over your soul like the balm of Gilead.

But can all the truths of prayer be summarized in a few short, simple sentences? Yes! They can be and they have been. Our Lord did it when He gave us the Lord's Prayer. As I said yesterday, the Lord's Prayer is a collection of index sentences covering every element of prayer. When you follow the words of this prayer sentence by sentence, principle by principle, you will find yourself covering every possible aspect of communicating with your Father in heaven. Every requirement for prayer, every element of worship and praise, every perspective of intercession and petition is covered in the Lord's Prayer. It is the true pattern for all prayer. Oh, what a treasure our Lord gave His disciples—and us—when they said, "Lord, teach us to pray."

Today we will begin looking at this pattern for prayer sentence by sentence. As we look at it one precept at a time, I will take you to other scriptures that amplify, illuminate, illustrate, or substantiate each particular precept.

I'm anxious for you to really dig into this study, Beloved. I don't want you to be merely a passive reader of truth. You need to actively participate in what you are learning. That is why I make this request: When you are asked to do something, please do it. Believe me, it won't be "busywork." Far from it! It will be a study that will help you seal truth to your heart and teach you to pray *doing* it.

Does it work? I know it does! We've taught all levels of inductive study, from our Discover 4 Yourself series for children to our 40-Minute Bible Studies with no required homework to Precept Upon Precept Bible Studies that take five hours a week. People have done it for years, for two generations now, teaching their children and children's children. And it has transformed lives and families because they are learning the Word of God for themselves—and His words are spirit and life, the very bread by which we live. Enough said—let's dig in.

THE TOPICS OF PRAYER

Yesterday you looked at the topics covered in the Lord's Prayer. For the sake of continuity, let me give you how I summarized the topics covered by the index sentences of Matthew 6:9-13.

The Sentence	The Topic
1. Our Father who is in heaven, hallowed be Your name.	*worship*
2. Your kingdom come.	*allegiance*
3. Your will be done, on earth as it is in heaven.	*submission*
4. Give us this day our daily bread.	*petition & provision*
5. And forgive us our debts, as we also have forgiven our debtors.	*confession & forgiveness*
6. And do not lead us into temptation, but deliver us from evil.	*watchfulness & deliverance*

7. For Yours is the kingdom   _____*worship*_____
   and the power and the
   glory forever. Amen.

Even though that last sentence is not in the earliest manuscripts but was added later, you can see how it brings prayer full circle, beginning and ending with the worship of God.

Although we may have worded our categories differently, I think we can all agree that the Lord's Prayer covers these basic and all-encompassing topics. Everything God's Word says on the subject of prayer can be aligned under one of these index sentences. What a gift of knowledge the Lord has given to us!

To pray according to the pattern of the Lord's Prayer is to cover every topic of prayer. It's a thorough work of prayer. But does this mean that every time you pray you cover all the topics—all the bases, so to speak?

DO I PRAY "THIS WAY" EVERY TIME I PRAY?

If you study all the times people communicated with God in prayer, you'll see that the answer to this question is no. You must be careful, then, not to impose something on yourself or others that God does not impose. As you may know, sometimes all we can do is cry "Oh Lord!" or "Help, Father."

In my own personal life (and yes, this is a confession), it seems I am constantly asking God to find something I've misplaced. When that happens, believe me, I don't cover all seven topics. You will, however, find me worshipping Him in the process. *Father, You're omniscient. You know where that thing is.* Then when it's found, I worship all over again! *Oh, thank You, Father, thank You.*

If you use the Lord's Prayer for what it is, the way to pray, it will not only keep you balanced when it comes to prayer, but it will also be an invaluable guide—a road map, so to speak. Often when I'm sitting in an airport, riding in the car with my husband, or lying in bed trying to wake up or go to sleep, I start praying sentence by sentence...

- lingering on each topic as the Lord leads, bringing those things on my heart to Him;
- beginning with worship but then turning to kingdom matters and submission to the will of God;
- calling out to the Father on behalf of my children and grandchildren, our staff, trainers, and students, that each might keep the kingdom before them and will to do His will;
- talking to Him about the world—that they will hunger for truth and for righteousness.

This, Beloved, is the practicality of knowing and using the Lord's Prayer. The Master Teacher, Jesus, covered it all in a brief and memorable way. In fact, it's meant to be memorized.

A Prayer to Be Memorized

If you don't know this prayer by heart, you really need to memorize it.

> **Read aloud Matthew 6:9-13 three times in a row every day (or sing it if you prefer). Hearing it is the key. It is easier to remember.**

> **Now write Matthew 6:9-13 on index cards, and then put them where you will be able to read them at strategic times during the day.**

You have just practiced two effective ways to memorize Scripture— methods you can use with other verses you want to commit to memory. By the way, when you memorize Scripture, may I suggest you use a word-for-word translation (for example, King James Version, New American Standard Bible, English Standard Version) rather than a phrase-by-phrase translation or a paraphrase? Value God's every word!

Do I Pray to God or to Jesus?

"Our Father..."

This is where all true prayer begins. It begins with God the Father, and it ends with God the Father. True prayer is nothing more and nothing less than communion with the Father. Whether you are involved in worship, intercession, petition, or thanksgiving, it is all directed to God the Father.

You often hear people pray, "Dear Jesus" or "Jesus." Yet should we direct our prayers to the Father or to the Son? Jesus Himself tells us to pray "Our Father." Yes, we come in the name of Jesus, for He is the One who gives us access to God through His death, burial, and resurrection; but it is all to bring us ultimately to the Father.

Now, then, one final word: When you come to God the Father in prayer, think about why you are coming to Him, what you believe about Him, and what is necessary on your part.

> **Read Hebrews 11:6 aloud. It is printed for you below.**
>
> *Without faith it is impossible to please Him, for he who comes to God must believe that He is and that He is a rewarder of those who seek Him.*
>
> **Now read this verse again out loud and answer these questions.**
>
> • **What are you to believe when you come to God in prayer?**
>
> _____
>
> _____
>
> _____

- Why are you coming to Him?

_____

_____

_____

- How are you to come to Him?

_____

_____

_____

It takes faith to approach God the Father and to please Him. And what is faith? It is defined in Hebrews 11:1: "Faith is the *assurance* of things hoped for, the *conviction* of things not seen" (emphasis added).

Prayer begins by communicating with a God who is there— although you have never seen Him. In light of all we have learned so far, can you see that the foundation, the fundamental truth of all prayer is faith in God? Those who come to Him must believe *He is*. He is what? He is God! And that He is a rewarder of those who seek Him. You come; He responds and rewards. Awesome! You have a God who exists and who cares; and who is omnipotent—able—that's why you come to Him. "What then shall we say to these things? If God is for us, who is against us? He who did not spare His own Son, but delivered Him over for us all, how will He not also with Him [Jesus] freely give us all things?" (Romans 8:31-32).

Wait! Don't go any further. Please take a moment to read those last two verses again. Think about them. Surely they tell you how precious you are to your heavenly Father. Worship Him. Thank Him for being there for you and for caring for all your needs. Worship is an essential ingredient to faith.

Oh, Beloved, do you see it? Jesus wants you to realize you are not coming to some remote, untouchable, indifferent Sovereign. You are coming to a Father—*our* Father!—a Father with children, a Father who loves, who cares, and who longs to have fellowship with His children—with you.

The question then becomes, "Is God truly your Father?"

According to God's Word, no man, woman, or child can call God "Father" apart from Jesus, for until we are born again God is not our Father (John 3:5). "As many as received Him [Jesus Christ], to them He gave the right to become children of God, even to those who believe in His name, who were born not of blood, nor of the will of the flesh nor of the will of man, but of God" (John 1:12-13).

You do not become a child of God until you receive the Lord Jesus Christ. Once you receive Him as your Lord and Savior, however, you are then sealed with the Holy Spirit. The Holy Spirit is given to you at salvation and is the guarantee of the redemption of your body. Look at Ephesians 1:13-14, which is printed out below and watch the progression of events. Underline the verbs.

> In Him, you also, after listening to the message of truth, the gospel of your salvation—having also believed, you were sealed in Him with the Holy Spirit of promise, who is given as a pledge of our inheritance, with a view to the redemption of God's own possession, to the praise of His glory.

Did you see it? I want to make sure you don't miss it, so bear with me. You hear—listen—to the message of truth, you believe what you hear, you are then sealed with the Holy Spirit. That means the Spirit of God comes to indwell you—live within you—and He, the Spirit becomes the guarantee of your redemption. The redemption of your body means you will have a brand-new body someday. One like Jesus' (1 John 3:2). This mortal will put on immortality (1 Corinthians 15:51-54).

Now, let me give you one last scripture that confirms it is only through salvation and the gift of the Holy Spirit that you can call God "Father." Romans 8:14-15 tells us, "All who are being led by the Spirit of God, these are sons of God…You have received a spirit of adoption as sons by which we cry out, 'Abba! Father!'"

God hears the words of all mankind—He's omnipresent (no hiding from Him) and omniscient (all knowing) and hears the cry of the seeking heart. However, prayer is privilege, the right, the inherent blessing reserved for those who are truly the children of God. Prayer is not the same for the masses who largely ignore God or who want Him on their terms except in dire cases of emergency; it is the birthright of those who can say with Jesus, "Our Father…"

Think about it. What significance does this have for your life?

I've had people share with me that one of the ways they discovered they had a religion rather than a relationship was the fact they never really had direct answers to prayer.

Many are in exactly this state, and my heart aches for them. The "something" that seems to be missing in their Christian experience, leaving it lifeless and routine, is really *Someone*—the blessed, indwelling Holy Spirit!

And how do you know if He is there—living within? His Spirit bears witness with your spirit (Romans 8:15-16). You know because there's a change in you! A Christian is a new creation.

If you have questions about the certainty of your salvation, Beloved, look up the following scriptures: 2 Corinthians 5:17; Ephesians 1:13-15; 1 John 2:3-6; 1 John 3:7-10; 1 Corinthians 6:9-11; and 1 John 5:11-14.

As you read these passages, ask God to speak to your heart, and then write down your observations. Ask Him to show you where you stand. You can have every confidence that He will, because He desires that you know truth, and He says that if you will search for Him with all your heart, you will be found by Him.

So what is the Spirit of God saying to you? Remember, He never condemns. It's not His will that you perish, but that you believe.

It's Time to Pray

If you want to move from a religion to a relationship, then tell God. Tell Him in your words. Tell Him you believe that Jesus is His Son and you want His Son to be your Lord, your Master, your Savior. Tell God you believe Jesus died for your sins—that you are a sinner in need of a savior. Tell Him that by faith you believe He raised His Son from the dead and that you desire to walk in newness of life. Write out your prayer below or simply write out, "I believe." Then write down the date—it's your "birthday"! The day you were born again, born from above, born of His Spirit.

_____

_____

_____

_____

_____

Now, if you are already saved, take a few minutes to talk to God just as a child would talk to his or her own earthly father.

"But, Kay," you may say, "my father never talked to me, never cared for me, so how can I talk to God as a father?" Even though you may not have had that kind of father, didn't you long for one who was loving, affectionate, caring, and accessible? Well, here He is, waiting for you to talk to Him.

Spill it all out...aloud. Tell God what you think about Him as a Father. Tell Him your fears, hopes, hesitations, and expectations. Tell Him what you long for in a relationship.

Remember the personal issues I asked you about in the introduction to this study? Lay those before Him if they are applicable. Then ask God what *He* longs for…and listen carefully for His answer.

Take note of what comes to your mind, giving Him time to speak. (If the thoughts are from God they will be in accord with His Word and His character.) Write those things you want to remember, things He brought to your mind, or what you cried out for.

_____

_____

_____

_____

_____

_____

Prayer Begins with Worship

Once you receive Jesus, you are not alone, and you will never be alone.

You are part of the family of God, and you have a Father who loves you more than you can begin to comprehend. Right from the beginning, Jesus makes that fact clear with the words "Our Father." Whether you are involved in worship, intercession, petition, or thanksgiving, it is all directed to God the Father.

If you desire to know Him as He truly is, you must go to the Word of God. Immediately you can see why so few really know Him, can't you? We will not know our Father or His ways intimately unless we are diligent students of His Word. Paul told Timothy,

> Be diligent to present yourself approved to God as a workman who does not need to be ashamed, accurately handling the word of truth (2 Timothy 2:15).

If we don't know our God and His ways, our prayers will be impotent and ineffective. We will not bring great things to our God in prayer unless we know how great *He* truly is. We will not ask God to move in the affairs of men in mighty ways until we understand His promises and His ways with the nations of the earth.

My heart's desire for everyone who reads these pages is to understand that the strength of our prayers begins in knowing our Father who is in heaven, and in realizing that "every good thing given and every perfect gift is from above, coming down from the Father of lights, with whom there is no variation or shifting shadow" (James 1:17).

Prayer belongs to those who are children of God—a family privilege. When we came to know God through Jesus Christ, God "rescued us from the domain of darkness, and transferred us to the kingdom of His beloved Son" (Colossians 1:13).

YOU'RE PART OF HIS "FOREVER FAMILY"

Consequently, "you are no longer strangers and aliens, but you are fellow citizens with the saints, and are of God's household" (Ephesians 2:19). Jesus told us that "'whoever does the will of My Father who is in heaven, he is My brother and sister and mother'" (Matthew 12:50). We are no longer "of your father the devil" (John 8:44). Ephesians 2 has some wonderful reminders. Read Ephesians 2:1-7. We are no longer "children of wrath" (verse 3), no longer "the sons of disobedience" (verse 2), no longer "dead in our transgressions" (verse 5). Rather, we have been made "alive together with Christ" (verse 5), "a dwelling of God in the Spirit" (verse 22). We are seated in heavenly places in Christ Jesus!

You are coming to a Father who loves you and desires your highest good:

> If you then, being evil, know how to give good gifts
> to your children, how much more will your Father
> who is in heaven give what is good to those who ask
> Him! (Matthew 7:11).

PRAYER BEGINS WITH WORSHIP

The very fact that you pray is an acknowledgement that God exists and that you need Him. Prayer demonstrates that you value God for who He is—the one true God, the One totally set apart from man, other than man, and more than man. He is God, the first and the last. Jehovah—LORD—the self-existent One (Genesis 2:4; Exodus 3:13-15; 6:3). There is no God besides Him (Isaiah 44:6).

And so it is, Beloved, when you come to God in prayer, you are coming to One greater and mightier than yourself, One whose memorial name to all generations is "I AM."

To worship God is to bow before Him, acknowledge His worth,

and give Him the honor and reverence due His holy name. A good way to remember the English meaning of worship is to think of looking at someone's worth. When we worship God, we rightly acknowledge God's worth, who He is, what He has done, and what He is able to do.

When you think about it, for prayer to begin and end with worship of the One who is in heaven—above the earth, above all—is only logical. The LORD who has "established His throne in the heavens" and whose "sovereignty rules over all" (Psalm 103:19) is able to do "according to His will in the host of heaven and among the inhabitants of earth" (Daniel 4:35). Worship correctly prepares us for all that follows in prayer.

Hallow (Not Hollow) His Name

Hallow is the word translated from the Greek *hagiazo*, which comes from *hagios*—to make holy, to set apart, to make a person or thing the opposite of common. To *hallow* God's name is to reverence it by believing He is who His Word says He is, and that He will always be and always do what He says.

God's name represents who God is. It reveals His character and attributes. The psalmist wrote, "You have magnified Your word according to all Your name" (Psalm 138:2). "According to" could be translated "together with." In other words, God's Word stands because God's name stands. One commentator writes, "The name of the Lord denotes not merely a title, but includes all that by which He makes Himself known and all that He shows Himself to be."

Do you remember God's commandment "You shall not take the name of the LORD your God in vain, for the LORD will not leave him unpunished who takes His name in vain" (Exodus 20:7)? Vain means "empty, worthless—hollow" rather than "hallowed."

The opposite of taking the Lord's name in vain is hallowing it! We take God's name in vain when we disbelieve, deny, or distort the truth about God. As I said earlier, God's names testify to His character. If you hallow His name, then you acknowledge and respect who He is and behave accordingly. When you and I refuse to believe God is who He says He is and will do what He says He will do, then we demean and defame Him.

In other words, we "hollow" our Father's name instead of hallowing it.

That's something to think about, isn't it? Many who would never think of taking the Lord's name in vain by cursing or by speaking it in a casual way still desecrate His name when they doubt, deny, or defame His character.

If you say, "I'm sorry, I just can't believe that God is the creator," or "I just can't believe God will really provide my needs," or "I just don't see why God would do that to a person," then you are not hallowing His name. You are taking His name in vain by thinking wrong thoughts about Him.

Let me share with you some of the names of God so you may revere Him as you should (see the chart on the next page). If you have time, you will find it of great benefit to look up and write down the Scripture references where these names are used so you might see the context in which God reveals each particular aspect of His character.

"Holy and awesome is His name" (Psalm 111:9). Meditate upon the names of God. Memorize them. Hallow them.

To assist you in studying the names of God in greater depth, you may want to use the study book entitled *Lord, I Want to Know You*.[1] I wrote this study on the names of God after I myself first studied the Lord's Prayer. I remember thinking, *Father, how can we fully hallow Your name if we don't know it?* That thought gave birth to that particular study, and it has been life-changing for multitudes of people as they learn who their God is and how to approach Him in prayer.

Read "The Names of God" chart carefully, paying attention to the various names of God and what they mean. When you have time, you will benefit

greatly by looking up the Scripture references where these names are used (perhaps writing them in the front or back of your Bible). Then you'll see the context in which God reveals each particular aspect of His character.

The Names of God

Name	Scripture	Means, or shows God as
Elohim	Genesis 1:1	Creator
El Elyon	Genesis 14:18-20	The Most High (Sovereign)
El Roi	Genesis 16:13	The God Who Sees
Adonai	Genesis 15:2	Lord, Master
El Shaddai	Genesis 17:1-3	The All-Sufficient One
Yahweh	Genesis 2:4; Exodus 6:2-4	Jehovah, the Self-Existent One
Jehovah-Tsidkenu	Jeremiah 23:6	The LORD Our Righteousness
Jehovah-Jireh	Genesis 22:14	The LORD Will Provide
Jehovah-Raah	Psalm 23:1	The LORD Is My Shepherd
Jehovah-Shalom	Judges 6:24	The LORD Is Peace
Jehovah-Nissi	Exodus 17:15	The LORD Is My Banner
Jehovah-Rapha (Rapa)	Exodus 15:26	The LORD Who Heals
Jehovah-Shammah	Ezekiel 48:35	The LORD Is There
Jehovah-Sabaoth	1 Samuel 1:3-11	The LORD of Hosts
Jehovah-Mekod-dishkem	Exodus 31:13	The Lord Who Sanctifies You

The stories of what God has done when individuals made His name their strong tower are miraculous—I'll share a couple with you in the pages to come. They will thrill you and encourage you to call on the name of the Lord in the day of trouble.

The Place of Worship in Prayer

Romans 15:4 tells us that what "was written in earlier times was written for our instruction." So there's much we can learn about prayer from Old Testament saints.

Look up the emphasized references in your Bible. Under each one (after I put it into context) note how the prayer begins—with worship, petition, and so forth. Then record how the individuals involved worshipped God, what they said or acknowledged about Him. Don't forget to mark any words for prayer.

Isaiah 37:14-20: Second Kings 18:13-37 tells that Sennacherib, the king of Assyria, was threatening to destroy Jerusalem if King Hezekiah would not surrender. You can find the same account in condensed form in Isaiah 37. It was a day of distress, rebuke, and rejection for Hezekiah, and he felt he had no strength to do anything about it (verse 3). Ever had a day like that? Is today a day like that? Read verses 14-20 and learn from him.

How prayer begins   How God is
                                   worshipped

_____   _____

_____   _____

_____   _____

2 Chronicles 20:3-19: It was another bad day in the land of Israel. Jehoshaphat, the king of Judah, had three armies coming against him, and he was afraid.

How prayer begins   How God is
worshipped

_____   _____

_____   _____

_____   _____

Acts 4:23-31: Peter and John healed a man and caused a stir (3:1-10). By declaring Jesus, they upset religious leaders who ordered them to quit preaching in Jesus' name (4:18).

How prayer begins   How God is
worshipped

_____   _____

_____   _____

_____   _____

Now, Beloved, stop and think about a day when you dealt with distress, rebuke, rejection, threats, or enemies. If it happens again, how can you apply what you have learned today?

When you find people worshipping the Godhead in Scripture, you never find them repeating the same phrases over and over again, such as, "Praise You, Jesus; praise You, Jesus; praise You, Jesus."

Yes, in Isaiah 6 you find the seraphim calling out, "Holy, Holy, Holy, is the LORD of hosts..." (Isaiah 6:3). A threefold repetition, however, was simply the way of denoting the ultimate of a truth, such as the holiness of God. A twofold repetition such as, "verily, verily" (or "truly, truly") established the veracity of something.

In biblical worship you do not find the repetition of a phrase; instead, you find the worshippers rehearsing the character of God and His ways, reminding Him of His faithfulness and His magnificent promises. The heathen often worked themselves up through excited and frenzied repetition of a phrase in the worship of their gods, but with the children of God this was not so!

In Matthew 6:7, preceding His teaching on the way to pray, Jesus admonished His disciples not to "use meaningless repetitions as the Gentiles do." Centuries later, John Wesley was used by God in the Great Awakening. Commenting on Jesus' Matthew 6 teaching, Wesley cautioned those he taught with these words,

> Do not use abundance of words without any meaning. Say not the same thing over and over again; think not the fruit of your prayers depends on the length of them...The thing here reproved is not simply the length, any more than the shortness of our prayers; but, length without meaning; speaking much, and meaning little or nothing.[2]

We do not need vain repetition. Our worship is based on truth, not emotion; it is based not on the fervency of our words, but on the faithfulness of our God. Emotion follows truth!

Turn to the following prayers in your Bible. As you read them, note how the petitioner worships God. By that I mean, what does he say about God? How does he approach God?

Jeremiah 32:16-25 _____

_____

Daniel 2:19-23 _____

_____

Daniel 9:3-19 _____

_____

Which do you think is more beneficial in worship:
a) simply repeating "Praise You, Jesus" over and
over; or b) rehearsing the character, the ways, and
the promises of your God? Which takes a greater
familiarity with God and His Word? If you were
the one being worshipped, which would you prefer?
Remember, to *worship* means to acknowledge
another's worth. Which form of worship does this
more effectively? Think about this in the light of
His Word and then worship your God accordingly.

It's Time to Pray

"Our Father who is in heaven." Spend time today worshipping
God—thinking of all you know, love, admire, and respect about
Him—and talk to Him about Who He is and what this means to
you personally. Also thank Him for opening your eyes to see truth,
thank Him for bringing you into His family. Tell Him what that
means to you and how deeply you appreciate the fact that Jesus
would die for your sins and that the Father, Son, and Spirit would
choose you for themselves, for their dwelling place.

Do it aloud, or write it down and then read your prayer of worship aloud.

First let me say that I am so proud of you for doing your home-work. At Precept Ministries International we are continually asking God to raise up men and women, teens and children, who are hungering and thirsting for a righteous life—a life lived according to the precepts of God.

We believe it is essential, imperative for you—whatever your age—to discover truth for yourself. Thank you for disciplining your-self for the purpose of godliness. You will never regret it.

Learning to pray God's way, according to His Word, becomes a pattern when we spend time with Him *every* day. Therefore we have a Saturday and Sunday assignment designed to help you include time with our Father over the weekend.

So what is your Saturday and Sunday assignment? It is to spend the weekend "hallowing His name." The more you do it, the more you will experience the truth of Proverbs 18:10: "The name of the LORD is a strong tower; the righteous runs into it and is safe."

On Saturday and then again on Sunday, choose one or more of God's names from the chart (page 47), a name or names that deal with where you are today. Look up the verse next to that name and then read the surrounding context so you know the setting in which that particular name of God is mentioned.*

Then call on that name, telling your heavenly Father you want to hallow His name by believing and living accordingly. Watch what God does in the days ahead as you become familiar with His vari-ous names.

---

* By the way, we have awesome children's inductive study courses on the Lord's Prayer (*Lord, Teach Me to Pray for Kids*) and on the names of God (*God, What's Your Name?*). They are in our Discover 4 Yourself series. For more information, see the back of this book. To order, you can either go online to www.precept.org or call us at 800-763-8280.

It's All About Him

Rehearsing the Character of God

Prayer begins with worship—focusing on God, rehearsing truth, calling on the One whom we know and trust. It's sad that many of us are so busy and stressed, so enamored and entangled with the world that we really don't know God as He wants us to know Him. Obviously, this has ramifications for our prayer life.

Some of us are more familiar with the New Testament than with the Old, but it's in the Old Testament that God introduces Himself. In page after page, He progressively reveals His person in His names, His character, His commandments, and His ways with people and nations. It is in the Old Testament that we develop our knowledge and understanding of God. Daniel 11:32 assures us that "the people who know their God will display strength and take action," or as the KJV says, "shall be strong, and do exploits."

Yet for many in today's world the appeal seems to be for "Bible lite."

People look for nondemanding, simplified Christian messages, heavy on application, loaded with feel-good stories, and easy on doctrine and Scripture.

In other words, *Nothing too hard, please. And keep it brief!*

As a result, when we come to "Our Father who is in heaven, hallowed be Your name," there's not always an abundance of truth in our treasure chest of praise and worship. Instead of coming to the Bible for a banquet, we're looking for an after-dinner mint.

Sometimes our thanksgiving, which is part of worship, comes up short as well. How can we "enter His gates with thanksgiving and His courts with praise" if we don't really know Him? How can we "give thanks to Him" and "bless His name" (Psalm 100:4) if we don't understand Him or His ways? How can we speak of "His faithful-ness to all generations" (verse 5)?

If we're not at home in the Word, it's difficult to turn to passages where we can rehearse His names, attributes, commandments, and promises, not to mention His dealings with people and nations.

If you are weak in the Word, Beloved, you will be weak in prayer.

If your knowledge of Scripture is shallow, your prayers will be too.

The two go hand in hand. The greatest book on prayer is the Bible. It should be our "book of common prayer."

Our lack of a true biblical knowledge of God can even show up in our worship music. Think of all the songs you can still sing—even the silly ones you learned from childhood! It's a vivid reminder that music can stay with us.

I believe many of the worship songs we sing repeatedly could benefit from stronger biblical content. We need to make certain we are worshipping in truth—singing choruses, songs, and hymns of biblical substance. Rather than seeking only a stirring of our emo-tions, we should concern ourselves first of all with transforming our minds to the mind of Christ. Just think what we could be engrafting in our hearts, minds, and souls if we sang songs of greater biblical depth.

The doctrine found in the first hymn ever penned by Isaac Watts is a strong example of what I'm talking about. Dissatisfied with the dismal singing at church, Isaac was challenged by his father to write his own music. And young Isaac did just that. As a 19-year-old, he wrote "Behold the Glories of the Lamb," based on the truths of Revelation 5:

> Behold the glories of the Lamb
> Amidst His Father's throne.
> Prepare new honors for His name,
> And songs before unknown.

Eternal Father, who shall look
Into Thy secret will?
Who but the Son should take that Book
And open every seal?

Now to the Lamb that once was slain
Be endless blessings paid;
Salvation, glory, joy remain
Forever on Thy head.

Thou hast redeemed our soul with blood,
Hast set the prisoners free;
Hast made us kings and priests to God,
And we shall reign with Thee.

Isaac's 600-plus hymns have lasted because they are built on eternal truths. Our worship should be founded—rooted, grounded—in *truth*, not emotion. Worship should be based on the goodness, faithfulness, wisdom, justice, and might of our eternal God. Emotion is natural, but genuine emotion follows truth! Power in prayer flows directly from our faith.

Worshipping God in Truth

Let's turn again to some prayers God has preserved for us in His Word and see what we can learn from others who worshipped God in truth (John 4:24). You do realize, don't you, that Jesus said the Father *seeks* such people to be His worshippers (verse 23)? Want to fill out a job application?

Let's look at three prayers of worship: Hannah's, Jeremiah's, and Daniel's. If you don't have time for all three, do at least one.

- Read each of the prayers in your Bible. Don't rush.
- Mark the references to prayer (don't forget the synonyms) in your Bible as you have done previously.

- Observe how the worshipper uses his or her knowledge of God in prayer, and see what you can learn.
- Under each Scripture reference, list what you learn about God—truths you want to remember about the One you are to worship in truth.

1 Samuel 2:1-10 _____

_____

Jeremiah 32:16-25 _____

_____

Daniel 2:19-23 _____

_____

It's Time to Pray

Take what you learned about God from the prayer(s) you just studied and write a prayer, poem, or song to worship God. You can do it! You're one of His much-loved, gifted children.

_____

_____

_____

_____

_____

Eagerly Awaiting Him

Your kingdom come," the second index sentence, is potent in its brevity.

But what does it mean? Why is it a topic for prayer? What is covered in this category of prayer? For a while I linked "Your will be done, on earth as it is in heaven" with "Your kingdom come." I couldn't see why these two sentences had to be separated. Understanding finally began to dawn after I'd meditated for a long time on these phrases.

"Your kingdom come"—or "May Your kingdom come," as we would say it less formally—is a confirmation in prayer of our allegiance to the sovereign rule of the kingdom of God above all else. It confirms our desire for God's visible rule upon the earth. The Jews, the people of Israel, awaited it. After the death and resurrection of Jesus Christ, Gentile believers joined them in watchful anticipation.

But somehow, I had missed it!

Although I was raised in church for the first 29 years of my life, I had never understood that Jesus would literally return to earth and set up His kingdom. I had a Bible, but I was blind to this truth because His Book bored me. The extent of my Bible knowledge came through hearing snippets of the Word on Sunday mornings, as portions of the Gospels and other Scriptures were read from both sides of the platform in front of the altar.

Along with the rest of the congregation, I recited the Apostles' Creed and the Lord's Prayer every Sunday without fail...and yet I had never come to an understanding that Jesus was coming again. Yes, I was in the church and loved it. I taught Sunday school, stayed active in the youth group, loved the church picnics and outings, and even dated one of the clergy who had been filling in for the summer; but I never knew that Jesus would return to rule and reign on planet Earth.

Nor did I hear that I had to be born again—believe on Jesus and personally receive Him, acknowledging Him as the Son of God and the only way to the Father. Baptized as an infant and confirmed at the age of 13, I thought I had arrived! I had never heard of a literal heaven, and most certainly knew nothing of a literal hell.

> Once I had no idea what I was saying when I prayed, "Your kingdom come." What about you? How I wish we could talk about these things face-to-face. It would be so wonderful to see your face, to hear your story, to reason through the Scriptures together. But since we can't, let me ask, "When you hear 'Your kingdom come,' what comes to mind?"

_____

_____

_____

_____

_____

> Do you think *worship* and *allegiance* are synonymous? Give the reason for your answer.

_____

_____

_____

_____

At this writing, I have just finished 55 television teaching programs in Israel on the Gospel of Matthew. What an experience—to teach Matthew in the very land where Jesus lived and taught its truths. It was an unforgettable experience for our entire team.

From his first words, Matthew established the fact that Jesus is the Messiah, the son of Abraham, the son of David, the One who will sit on the throne of David and whose kingdom will have no end. Then he began to tell us what His kingdom is all about as John the Baptist came preaching, "Repent, for the kingdom of heaven is at hand" (Matthew 3:2). Jesus followed John, preaching, going throughout all Galilee proclaiming the gospel of the kingdom.

In the Sermon on the Mount, Jesus told His hearers to whom the kingdom of heaven belongs. And in teaching them how to pray, Jesus told us to pray that the Father's kingdom would come, and that His will would be done on earth as it is done in heaven. (I could go on and on walking us through Matthew, reading of Christ's return, the setting up of His throne on earth, and the drinking again of the fruit of the vine with His faithful disciples in the kingdom.) And then we come to the final words of the Gospel, Jesus' commission to the Eleven. (Eleven because one had defected. Judas had not given his allegiance to Jesus.)

Let's read Jesus' closing words as they are printed out below. Put a box around *authority*.

Jesus came up and spoke to them, saying, "All authority has been given to Me in heaven and on earth. Go therefore and make disciples of all the nations, baptizing them in the name of the Father and the Son and the Holy Spirit, teaching them to observe all that I commanded you; and lo, I am with you always, even to the end of the age" (Matthew 28:18-20).

Let's observe what you marked.

- Whose authority?

_____

_____

- How did He get it?

_____

_____

- How extensive is that authority?

_____

_____

- Where does it reach or what does it cover?

_____

_____

- How much authority does He have?

_____

_____

- What is the basis of Jesus' command to the disciples? (Hint: When you see a "therefore," find out what it's there for.)

_____

_____

The kingdom of God is all about His authority over us, over all mankind. There is one God—only one—and it's not you or me! And because He alone is God, I owe my total allegiance to Him and no other.

> **Do you know people who acknowledge the worship of God yet do not seem fully aligned with His kingdom and its preeminence? What things appear to take priority in their lives?**

> _____

> _____

> _____

> **Over what do those things seem to take precedence?**

> _____

> _____

> _____

> **How is this priority manifested in the way they live?**

> _____

> _____

> _____

It's one thing to make an accurate declaration of who God is, and another thing entirely to give God our full allegiance. I know people who can go on and on about God's attributes and eternal glory, and yet their actual allegiance is to the furtherance of their own ambitions, welfare, creature comforts, luxuries, education, and personal advancement—or to a narrow, legalistic set of do's and don'ts.

I know people who say, "I know I should study God's Word more," or "I know I should witness," or "I know I should give more," or "I know I should be more involved in His work, but…"

But *what?* What are they really saying? Record your thoughts.

_____

_____

_____

I think in reality they are saying (though not in so many words), "But my first allegiance is not to God." Think about it. And think about where *you* are in life, Beloved.

"But Kay," you may say, "doesn't allegiance fit right in with submission to His will when we pray, 'Your will be done'?" Yes, the two do go together. But true, complete, absolute submission to God's will is born only out of undivided, absolute allegiance to His kingdom.

Unfortunately, many of us—even those who attend church and profess Christianity or a belief in God—have fallen flat on our faces in the mud of this present world. Instead of living in total obedience, unwavering allegiance to His kingdom and His reign as King in our lives, we are double-minded, desiring the best of both worlds. We forget that "our citizenship is in heaven, from which also we eagerly wait for a Savior, the Lord Jesus Christ" (Philippians 3:20).

We are not eagerly awaiting Him because we have entangled ourselves in the affairs of everyday life and have forgotten we are to please the one who enlisted us as soldiers (see 2 Timothy 2:4). Too often our allegiances are to money and what it provides, to position and its prestige, to material possessions and pleasures, and even to "churchianity" and its works.

Notice I say *churchianity,* not Christianity.

There is such a difference, Beloved.

Churchianity puts people first; church is about them and their desires. *Christianity* puts Christ in His rightful place as head of the church.

Let's face it, too often in life our walk doesn't match our talk. We want only enough of Christianity to get us to heaven, only enough to get our prayers answered and get the benefits of healing and prosperity. We don't want to give total allegiance to His kingdom, because it calls us to a cross. We don't want His kingdom to come today, tomorrow, or even within a few years because, like Demas, we love this present world more (2 Timothy 4:10).

Is this right or is it wrong? Does any of it describe you?

I don't mean to sound harsh, Beloved, but as I write, this truth is "in my heart...like a burning fire shut up in my bones" (Jeremiah 20:9). Oh, how my heart grieves as I see so many who name His name yet have not given Him their total allegiance. Oh, how my heart grieves when the Spirit of God shows me incidents in my own life where I have failed to give my absolute, total, unwavering allegiance to Him, the Lord God of all heaven and earth.

"Kay," you might say, "you are judging." No, Beloved, I am *discerning.* Do you realize that God calls us to discern? Study Matthew 7 carefully, and you will see that our fruit—our doing or not doing of the Word—bears witness to our allegiance.

When people have time for everything except a personal, diligent study of God's Word, we know they are not "approved to God" as Paul spoke of in 2 Timothy 2:15. They know much about the world but little about their Lord. Why? Because they have time for the things of this life, but can't seem to find any time at all to study God's Word. They refuse to believe that "man shall not live on bread alone, but on every word that proceeds out of the mouth of God" (Matthew 4:4). Communion with God through His Word and prayer is essential to the fruitful life that will hasten the coming of His kingdom.

Filling in the words of the first two index sentences, following our example of the One who tells us how

to pray, is good review for your memorization of
the Lord's Prayer.

"Our _____."

Now, open your Bible to Matthew 4:8-10. Mark each
reference to the devil. I use a red pitchfork like this
⚡ . Don't miss the pronouns as you read.

• What was the devil offering Jesus in this passage?

_____

_____

• How does Jesus' response line up with the first two
index sentences of the Lord's Prayer?

_____

_____

_____

Now let's think. Scripture tells us that the devil is
also our adversary. How might he tempt us in a
similar way?

_____

_____

_____

• What should be our answer?

_____

When Jesus calls men and women to Himself, for what kind of allegiance does He ask? Carefully read these scriptures and 1) circle or color every reference to those to whom Jesus is speaking; 2) underline or use a different color to show everything the person is told to do.

Mark 8:34-35:

> 34 He summoned the crowd with His disciples, and said to them, "If anyone wishes to come after Me, he must deny himself, and take up his cross and follow Me.
>
> 35 "For whoever wishes to save his life will lose it, but whoever loses his life for My sake and the gospel's will save it."

Luke 14:25-27:

> 25 Now large crowds were going along with Him; and He turned and said to them,
>
> 26 "If anyone comes to Me, and does not hate his own father and mother and wife and children and brothers and sisters, yes, and even his own life, he cannot be My disciple.
>
> 27 "Whoever does not carry his own cross and come after Me cannot be My disciple."

Matthew 10:37-39:

> 37 "He who loves father or mother more than Me is not worthy of Me; and he who loves son or daughter more than Me is not worthy of Me.
>
> 38 "And he who does not take his cross and follow after Me is not worthy of Me.

39 *"He who has found his life will lose it, and he who has lost his life for My sake will find it."*

Matthew 6:33:

33 *"Seek first His kingdom and His righteousness, and all these things will be added to you."*

Anything less than denying yourself, taking up your cross, and following Him (Mark 8:34), "hating" your family and even your own life,[3] seeking His kingdom first—anything less is divided allegiance. Anything less will not allow you to honestly pray, "Your kingdom come." Therefore, when you pray, "Your kingdom come," examine yourself to see whether anything in your heart is keeping you from undivided allegiance to the coming of His kingdom.

It's Time to Pray

Oh, Beloved, why don't you go to our Father and ask Him to show you anything that might be dividing or dissipating your allegiance to His kingdom? Write it down.

_____

_____

_____

Then, if you feel that you might slip back into this competing allegiance, confess this to your spouse or to a close and faithful friend in the Lord, and together seek God in prayer. Ask this individual to hold you accountable. As Scripture tells us,

Two are better than one because they have a good return for their labor. For if either of them falls, the one will lift up his companion. But woe to the one who falls when there is not another to lift him up (Ecclesiastes 4:9-10).

For the Sake of the Kingdom

The itinerant evangelist's heart brimmed over with joy as he made his way to the sixth village on his journey. It was Christmas. Having seen a number of Chinese come to believe in Jesus, he was anticipating the same success in this village.

"Greetings," he called to a group of villagers. "I am bearer of good news." Before the evangelist could go on, however, a man interrupted him.

"We have only bad news here," he said irritably. "A couple has just had their baby stolen." (Kidnapping and selling babies is not uncommon in China.)

As the evangelist shared their sorrow he said, "I know someone who can help you—God. Let me pray to Him on your behalf." There was no reaction on their sad faces. "Yet," as he later wrote, "I went into prayer anyway, feeling very uncomfortable: 'Dear Father, many years ago at this same time of year You sent a child into the world and rescued us all. I ask that You bring back this man's child and deliver this village from sadness.'"

Suddenly the young father of the stolen child spoke out. "Shut up and go away. We have prayed to our gods and nothing has happened. Why should yours be any different?"

The people propelled the evangelist from the village. His Christmas joy turned to sorrow. He felt like a total failure as he made his way down the road in a daze of humiliation and tears. Then he remembered Jesus—His commission to go and make disciples, His rejection, and His willingness to suffer in order to accomplish the will of His Father.

Though frightened, for the sake of the kingdom of God the evangelist turned and walked slowly back to the village. His heart wouldn't let him do anything else. As the afternoon sun began its descent, he heard the cry of a baby from the shaft of a well. The baby's face was blue, its little bottom uncovered. Then he understood. When the captors discovered the baby was a girl, she was abandoned in the well. Girls were of no value. Those who purchased kidnapped babies wanted only boys.

When the people of the village saw him carrying the baby, they came running—the mother among them. The smile on her face seemed almost holy. "Come and warm yourself by our fire," the father said. "Who was that God you prayed to?"

Allegiance to the kingdom of God brought the evangelist back, and God opened their hearts to believe.

FURTHERING THE KINGDOM OF GOD

When you and I pray, "Your kingdom come," we are asking God to further His kingdom. Yes, to bring His visible rule upon the earth in days to come, but also to bring it to the hearts of mankind *now*, in these last days—days that began with the first coming of His Son (Hebrews 1:2) and which will end with His Son's second coming. The gospel comes individually before it comes globally.

> Write what Jesus said in Matthew 24:14 about the gospel of the kingdom. (I color code references to God's kingdom like this ♔.)

> Read Matthew 24:30 and 25:31 and record what you learn. The "end" references the end of the present age brought about when Jesus Christ...

> _____

> _____

> _____

> _____

By the way, I mark every reference to the second coming of Jesus Christ with a cloud like this: ⟨cloud⟩ . Then I color the center yellow and the rest, light blue.

What does Revelation 14:6-7 tell us about the proclamation of the gospel? As you write your answer below, notice who does what, for whom, and when it will happen.

Since the event described in this passage will occur someday, what is our responsibility today? Who is to declare the good news of the gospel until then? Do you remember Jesus' words as recorded in Matthew 28:19-20? We looked at them earlier.

> Go therefore and make disciples of all the nations, baptizing them in the name of the Father and the Son and the Holy Spirit, teaching them to observe all that I commanded you; and lo, I am with you always, even to the end of the age.

Read them again and double underline "make disciples," the sentence's main verb. "Go" (literally "as you are going"), "baptizing," and "teaching" are participles supporting the main verb (in the Greek). Put a squiggly line under them.

So what is our task as believers in Jesus Christ?

_____

_____

Making disciples begins with sharing the gospel. And what is the gospel? Can you remember what we learned in our first week of study? List below the two main points we saw in 1 Corinthians 15. You need to know and remember these things if you are going to proclaim them!

1. _____

2. _____

DEBTORS TO THE GOSPEL

Just before Jesus ascended to heaven, His disciples asked Him a question. Read Acts 1:6-8 and answer the following questions:

• What were the disciples asking Jesus?

_____

_____

_____

• What was His answer?

_____

_____

_____

• According to verse 8, what were the disciples to be?

_____

_____

- **Where were they to do this?**

_____

_____

Jesus will restore the kingdom to Israel when He returns as King of kings and sits on David's throne. But until that time the followers of Jesus Christ have a mission and commission. Why? Because men and women are born in sin and will perish if they don't receive forgiveness of their sins by believing in Jesus Christ.

Never forget that, Beloved.

There is salvation in no other (Acts 4:12).

Romans 10 makes it clear that people cannot believe in someone of whom they have never heard. They must hear, and for that reason alone, we must share. This is why Paul saw himself as a debtor to the gospel. In Romans 1:16 Paul wrote that the gospel is the power of God for salvation to all who believe, to the Jew first and then the Greek (all who are not Jews). And we are debtors!

PRAYER IS KINGDOM WORK

When we pray, "Your kingdom come," we are about kingdom work—getting the gospel to the lost. The kingdom cannot come until His body is complete, until the last of His sheep is brought into the fold, for He will not lose one of His own (John 10):

> The Lord is not slow about His promise [to return
> and set up His kingdom], as some count slowness,
> but is patient toward you, not wishing for any to
> perish but for all to come to repentance (2 Peter 3:9).

What do we conclude from this passage? When you pray for the coming of His kingdom, you are "hastening the coming of the day of God" (verse 12).

The world is on God's heart, and needs to be on our hearts as well. It's on your knees, precious one, that you make your commitment, bowing before Him, honoring your Father as your God, and making yourself available as His ambassador wherever He sends you. It is on your knees that you water the soil of men's hearts through prayer, so the ground is ready to receive the seed of His word.

Would you get on your knees now and simply say to God, "Father, my allegiance is to You alone. May Your kingdom come"?

Adrian Rogers was a pastor at Bellevue Baptist Church in Cordova, Tennessee, for 32 years. He and his wife, Joyce, whom I love and admire, lived passionately for God's kingdom, faithful unto his death. I can close my eyes right now and hear him say,

> No matter how faithfully you attend church, how generously you give, how circumspectly you walk, how eloquently you teach, or how beautifully you sing, if you are not endeavoring to bring people to Jesus Christ, you are not right with God.

Is your unwavering allegiance also to the kingdom of God?

It's Time to Pray

Thoughtfully read this quote from A.B. Simpson:

> There is no ministry that will bring more power and blessing than the habit of believing, definite, and persistent prayer for the progress of Christ's kingdom, for the needs and work of His church, for His ministers and servants, and especially for the evangelization of the world and the vast neglected myriads who know not how to pray for themselves.

Be encouraged to pray as you put into practice what you've learned in these first two index—topical—sentences. In preparation for prayer, first list several truths you know about your heavenly Father, the kingdom of God, and the gospel of Jesus Christ. You might want to write them down.

_____

_____

_____

_____

Then worship Him according to what you know about Him. For instance, you might write that He loves the world so much that He gave His Son. You would then take that truth and pray something like this:

> Oh Father, I thank You for loving me, for loving people
> so very much that You sent Your very own Son to
> earth to die for all mankind. Thank You, Jehovah-
> Jireh, for providing Jesus as the sacrifice for my sins
> and for the sins of the whole world.

Giving your allegiance to God might sound something like this:

> Father, I know that I am to share this good news with
> others, and that thought scares me. But if You will
> help me, if You will open the doors of opportunity, I
> will walk through them. I want to be obedient. And
> Father, would You go before me by Your Spirit and
> prepare the hearts of the people with whom I share? I
> think especially of my neighbors, Lord. Their family is
> hurting so badly. They are on the verge of divorce, and
> I know it's not Your will. Show me how to help and
> encourage them.

From there you might pray for a country; for those who suffer illness or abuse; for Muslims, Hindus, Buddhists, and so forth. Pray for those whom God by His Spirit lays on your heart.

As you pray, Beloved, pray aloud. Confessing truth and hearing ourselves pray seals and confirms our prayers in our hearts and minds. It also helps keep our thoughts from wandering.

Finally, Beloved, pray, "Come, Lord Jesus" (Revelation 22:20). *Your kingdom come.*

A Heart Attitude for Today

Your will be done, on earth as it is in heaven."
This phrase follows the declaration of allegiance to God's kingdom. Our hearts long for the reign of God on the earth, the end of blatant sin, blasphemy, rebellion, and man's inhumanity to man. We long for the earth to be filled with the knowledge of the Lord as the waters cover the sea, for every knee to bow and every tongue to confess Jesus Christ for who He truly is. We cherish the fact that Jerusalem will be a praise in all the earth and all the nations will come to see God's glory. Yes, this is our first and rightful thought as we pray, "Your will be done, on earth as it is in heaven."

But what can we conclude here? Is this a prayer that applies only to that future day when Jesus returns? Does "Your will be done, on earth as it is in heaven" make reference only to that great day when "the sovereignty, the dominion and the greatness of all the kingdoms under the whole heaven will be given to the people of the saints of the Highest One," when "all the dominions will serve and obey Him" (Daniel 7:27)?

A PRAYER FOR THE PRESENT

"Your will be done" is a prayer that applies to much more than the coming kingdom and the coming age. *It is a heart attitude of submission to the sovereignty and will of the Father.*

If you want to pray correctly and have your prayers answered by God, you must be willing to do His will *now*—while the entire world lies in the power of the evil one (1 John 5:19), opposing God's truth and reign.

First and foremost, what is God's work and God's will? Read the following verses and box or color

every occurrence of the words *work* and *will*. Then underline what the work or will of God is.

> Jesus answered and said to them, "This is the work of God, that you believe in Him whom He has sent" (John 6:29).

John 6:38-40:

> 38 "I have come down from heaven, not to do My own will, but the will of Him who sent Me.
>
> 39 "This is the will of Him who sent Me, that of all that He has given Me I lose nothing, but raise it up on the last day.
>
> 40 "For this is the will of My Father, that everyone who beholds the Son and believes in Him will have eternal life, and I Myself will raise him up on the last day."

Now, Beloved, read the following three passages and circle every occurrence of *believe, believes,* and *believing*. Then underline what happens to those who believe or don't believe.

John 12:44-46:

> 44 Jesus cried out and said, "He who believes in Me, does not believe in Me but in Him who sent Me.
>
> 45 "He who sees Me sees the One who sent Me.
>
> 46 "I have come as Light into the world, so that everyone who believes in Me will not remain in darkness."

John 16:8-9:

> 8 "He [speaking of the Spirit of God], when

He comes, will convict the world concern-
ing sin and righteousness and judgment;
9 *"concerning sin, because they do not believe*
in Me."

These have been written so that you may
believe that Jesus is the Christ, the Son of God;
and that believing you may have life in His
name (John 20:31).

The work of God is that you believe on the Lord Jesus Christ whom God has sent (see John 6:40). He is God incarnate, or God "in the flesh." And that describes the Lord Jesus; He is God in the flesh (John 1:1-2,14). In other words, the Father's will is that you believe that Jesus Christ who has come in the flesh, born of a virgin (Matthew 1:20-25) and without sin (2 Corinthians 5:21), is God—I Am. Not to believe this truth is to die in your sins (John 8:24).

Those who do not believe in the Lord Jesus Christ are sinning (John 16:9), going directly against the will of God. For that reason, they remain dead in trespasses and sins (Ephesians 2:1). The wrath of God abides on them (John 3:36), for "there is salvation in no one else; for there is no other name under heaven that has been given among men by which we must be saved" (Acts 4:12).

Read the above paragraph one more time. If it con-
tains anything you do not believe, cross it out in the
paragraph. Then go to the "address" of that truth
in the Bible—book, chapter, and verse—and cross it
out of your Bible. Write why you don't believe it.

_____

_____

_____

_____

_____

_____

The Lord's Prayer is God's way for believers to pray. Jesus' first words confirm this: "Our Father." We know from John 8:44 and others that there are only two fathers and that each human being belongs to one of them: the devil or God.

As you have seen, salvation is submission to truth—believing it, aligning yourself under it. As a liar and the father of lies (John 8:44), the devil will nevertheless speak truth at times if it suits his evil purposes (see Matthew 4:6). God is truth; Jesus is the truth (John 14:6). To believe that Jesus is God is to acknowledge His position and rights as God. To recognize Him as Savior is to see that only this God-man can save you from your sins. Jesus took on flesh and blood so that He might taste death for every person (Hebrews 2:9).

Reason with Me Now

Come and let's think this through. What is the root of all sin?

It is independence. Think of the first words of the serpent of old: "Has God said?" "You will be like God…"

It is self, walking its way—demanding its own way.

Isaiah 53:6 says that like sheep we have turned each "to his own way." If you look up the verses that actually define sin, you discover that each verse shows to one degree or another that we have willfully chosen to break the law, to not believe, to walk our own path rather than God's.

One of the evidences of salvation is a willingness to submit to God—to recognize that because He is God and you are His creation, you are to bow your knee in surrender and accept Him as Lord. Before we pursue this attitude of submission and its application to prayer, however, let's look at the relationship of submission and salvation.

In your Bible observe Matthew 7:21-27 carefully, and answer these questions (watch for the word "will"):

- Who will enter the kingdom of heaven?

_____

- Whose house will stand through the storms, and why?

_____

- How did Jesus describe those He said He never knew? What were they doing?

_____

_____

_____

- According to verse 22, does what they did show they were saved and bound for heaven?

_____

- Why would they be denied entrance to the kingdom of heaven?

_____

- Whose house fell and why?

_____

- Where is submission is all this?

_____

- With which of these two groups do you identify?

_____

- Look up John 9:31 in your Bible and write it below.

_____

_____

_____

- Based on this verse, whom does God not hear?

_____

- Whom *does* God hear, and why?

_____

- What does this have to do with submission?

_____

_____

If you and I are *not* willing to say to God in prayer, "Your will be done, on earth as it is in heaven," can we expect our prayers to be answered? Whew! That's something to really stop and think about, isn't it?

It's Time to Pray

Are you still in your sins, or are you a worshipper of God who longs to do the will of the Father? Only the latter has access to God in prayer. May I suggest that you spend some time in prayer talking to the Father about His will? List any area of life where you have not submitted to the will of God.

_____

_____

_____

_____

May I make one more suggestion? If you are physically able, get flat on your face before God on the floor and spread out your hands, so that your body takes the form of a cross. In that position pray, "Your will be done on earth—*now, in me*—as it is in heaven."

Our Greatest Example

The One who teaches us to pray, "Your will be done on earth, as it is in heaven," is our greatest Example of submission to the will of God.

Let's go together and stand on some sacred ground...the garden of Gethsemane. While each Gospel records the events of that sorrowful night, Matthew elaborates on the prayers of our Savior at that time.

> **As you read Matthew 26:36-44, which is printed out below...**
>
> - **mark or color in a distinctive color every reference to prayer.**
>
> - **put a circle around every reference to time, along with a squiggly line. I draw an old-fashioned clock over references to time in my Bible, and then put a squiggly line under the entire reference to time. For example, I mark "a second time" like this.** 🕐
>
> - **put a box around those words Jesus used to refer to the will of God, or highlight them with yellow.**

Matthew 26:36-44:

> *36 Jesus came with them to a place called Gethsemane, and said to His disciples, "Sit here while I go over there and pray."*
> *37 And He took with Him Peter and the two sons of Zebedee, and began to be grieved and distressed.*

38 Then He said to them, "My soul is deeply grieved, to the point of death; remain here and keep watch with Me."

39 And He went a little beyond them, and fell on His face and prayed, saying, "My Father, if it is possible, let this cup pass from Me; yet not as I will, but as You will."

40 And He came to the disciples and found them sleeping, and said to Peter, "So, you men could not keep watch with Me for one hour?

41 "Keep watching and praying that you may not enter into temptation; the spirit is willing, but the flesh is weak."

42 He went away again a second time and prayed, saying, "My Father, if this cannot pass away unless I drink it, Your will be done."

43 Again He came and found them sleeping, for their eyes were heavy.

44 And He left them again, and went away and prayed a third time, saying the same thing once more.

What do you learn from marking the references to prayer?

_____

_____

_____

_____

What did Jesus pray?

_____

_____

_____

_____

What do you learn from marking the references to time?

_____

_____

_____

_____

Do you think this was easy for Jesus? After all, as God, He knew very well what was about to happen. Before you answer, look at what Luke told us in Luke 22:41-44. Write your discovery in the space provided.

_____

_____

_____

Now, look at three other scriptures that chronologically lead up to Luke 22. Read them carefully and record what they tell you about Jesus' knowledge of and submission to the will of God.

"The Son of Man has come to seek and to save that which was lost" (Luke 19:10).

"Now My soul has become troubled; and what shall I say, 'Father, save Me from this hour'? But for this purpose I came to this hour. Father, glorify Your name" (John 12:27-28).

John 17:1-4:

1 *Jesus spoke these things; and lifting up His eyes to heaven, He said, "Father, the hour has come; glorify Your Son, that the Son may glorify You,*

2 *"even as You gave Him authority over all flesh, that to all whom You have given Him, He may give eternal life.*

3 *"This is eternal life, that they may know You, the only true God, and Jesus Christ whom You have sent.*

4 *"I glorified You on the earth, having accomplished the work which You have given Me to do."*

Jesus knew why He had come—to be the Lamb of God who would take away the sins of the world. But at what a cost! The price to be paid was horrendous: death, separation from His Father! For the first and only time in all of eternity, the Father would forsake His Son—because the wages of sin is death, and death is separation from God. As we know, Jesus would cry, "My God, My God, why have You forsaken me?" (Matthew 27:46). Yet it was the will of God—the kernel of wheat would have to die or it would abide alone. For this reason He could not say, "Save Me from this hour." It was for this hour He had come. He had been born to die, and He would not turn back. He would glorify the Father, and accomplish the work God had given Him to do.

This, Beloved, is the One who tells us to pray, "Your will be done."

Can you see how God progressively brings us to this point in prayer? First, we acknowledge who God is and honor Him accordingly: "Our Father who is in heaven, hallowed be Your name." Then, we give Him our allegiance: "Your kingdom come." And third, we tell Him we want His will to be done here on earth in us as it is done in heaven.

The work of the kingdom is accomplished by our submission and obedience to the will of God. Kingdom work cannot be done apart from doing what God desires. "We are His workmanship, created in Christ Jesus for good works, which God prepared beforehand so that we would walk in them" (Ephesians 2:10).

Precious child of God, do you realize this? Do you believe this? Will you pray accordingly? Pause for a few minutes and talk to your Father about these truths.

As you surrender yourself to know and do His will, you'll want to pray the same thing for others. I often use Paul's prayer in Colossians 1:9-12.

Let's study Paul's prayer, and then we'll pray. As you read,

- **mark the references to prayer.**
- **put a box around the reference to His will.**
- **color "knowledge" green.**

Colossians 1:9-12:

> 9 ...We have not ceased to pray for you
> and to ask that you may be filled with
> the knowledge of His will in all spiritual
> wisdom and understanding,
> 10 so that you will walk in a manner worthy
> of the Lord, to please Him in all respects,
> bearing fruit in every good work and
> increasing in the knowledge of God;
> 11 strengthened with all power, according to

His glorious might, for the attaining of all
steadfastness and patience; joyously
12 *giving thanks to the Father, who has quali-*
fied us to share in the inheritance of the
saints in Light.

Why did Paul want them to be filled with the knowledge of God's will? Record your thoughts here or on the next page.

_____

_____

_____

Number the things in verses 10-12 (beginning with "so that you will walk") that are to show forth from our lives. For example, I put a circled 1 above *to please*. You continue with 2, 3, and so forth.

10 *so that you will walk in a manner worthy*
   of the Lord, to please Him in all respects,
   bearing fruit in every good work and
   increasing in the knowledge of God;
11 *strengthened with all power, according to*
   His glorious might, for the attaining of all
   steadfastness and patience; joyously
12 *giving thanks to the Father, who has quali-*
   fied us to share in the inheritance of the
   saints in Light.

It's Time to Pray

Today simply pray Colossians 1:9-12 aloud, mentioning the name of the person(s) you want to pray for wherever you see a "you." Do you know what is so valuable about praying Scripture? You are praying according to the Word and will of God. Don't give up…give God time to work His good work in their lives.

Be like the persistent friend Jesus used as an illustration in Luke 11. Keep on asking and it will be given to you, keep on seeking and you will find, keep on knocking and it will be opened (Luke 11:5-10; Matthew 7:7). "Ask," "seek," and "knock" in Matthew 7:7 are all in the present tense in the Greek, which implies continuous or habitual action. Persevere, my friend.

L earning to pray God's way, according to His Word, becomes a pattern when we spend time with Him every day. That is why this weekend exercise is important. Remember the title of this book is *Lord, Teach Me to Pray in 28 Days*. We can't skip the weekend! We need to communicate with God daily—continually, about everything—so let me give you another weekender.

Let's think about what competes for our allegiance to God. Sometimes it is the "worries of the world...the deceitfulness of riches and the desires for other things" (Mark 4:19). Read Matthew 6:24-34 aloud this Saturday and Sunday. Read it slowly, thoughtfully. Ask God to search your heart with the light of His Word. Then stop and think about what you read. "You cannot serve God and wealth" (6:24). Does that statement hit home? Pierce your heart in any way? Trouble your conscience? Do you feel like your allegiance to God has in any way been compromised in your desire for the things of this world? Or possibly in the anxieties of life? If so, talk to your Father about it.

Also, you might want to mark every reference to not worrying in verses 25-34. Check yourself out there. Write down anything you are worrying about. Then remember we are coming to that topical sentence "Give us this day our daily bread." You have already seen it. Therefore, when you finish your list, see if there are any scriptures you know that would take care of these worries—cover them with a promise. If so, take that promise to God and remember what you just saw in Matthew 6:33-34. You do your part and let God do His!

Blessings to you, Beloved of God...and me!

Week Three

You Belong to God

Our Prayers Connect Heaven and Earth

Have you ever finished your prayer time feeling like it was nothing?

Of course you have, and so have I.

It can be so frustrating! After such times my emotions have varied from a feeling of total impotence, to guilt (because of a wandering mind), to a sense of near despair. I have wondered, *Father, will I ever learn to really pray—and cover everything that needs to be covered in prayer?*

Surely Jesus sensed this would happen to us, for prayer is probably the most disciplined and difficult exercise in the Christian's life. Oh, how I love this God of ours who has truly promised to supply all of our needs...even our need in prayer. How I thank Him for opening my eyes to see what Jesus was doing when He said, "Pray, then, in this way" (Matthew 6:9).

It has been so exciting to realize that the Lord's Prayer is an index prayer, a collection of brief sentences, each suggesting a subject of prayer. Now we know *how* to pray—how to "cover all the bases." All we have to do is recite one sentence of this prayer at a time, realize what topic or point it covers, and then simply talk to the Father about anything that falls under that particular part of the index. When we finish the first point, we move on to the second.

To go through the entire collection of index sentences is to cover the whole expanse of prayer. Or as G. Campbell Morgan, the prince of expositors, said,

> To pray that prayer intelligently is to have nothing
> else to pray for. It may be broken up, each petition

may be taken separately and expressed in other ways, but in itself, it is exclusive and exhaustive.

My heart brims over with joy and praise as I think of these things. *Oh, Father, thank You, thank You, thank You for this instruction from Your Son!*

Do you see, Beloved? Memorize the Lord's Prayer, and no one can take from you God's way to pray. You will have it for the rest of your life. From the youngest babe in Christ to the most mature saint, here is the way you can pray and know that your prayers are pleasing to God. And it's a form of prayer that will expand as you deepen in your knowledge of and walk with Him.

When you take time to study the Lord's Prayer carefully, you will begin to pick up on a change of direction in the pattern of prayer. Read Matthew 6:9-13 to see if you can discover this change for yourself.

Mark the references to God, including "Your," in one color or way. Highlight the references to "us" and "we" in a different color.

> 9 *"Pray, then, in this way: 'Our Father who is in heaven, hallowed be Your name.*
> 10 *'Your kingdom come. Your will be done, on earth as it is in heaven.*
> 11 *'Give us this day our daily bread.*
> 12 *'And forgive us our debts, as we also have forgiven our debtors.*
> 13 *'And do not lead us into temptation, but deliver us from evil. [For Yours is the kingdom and the power and the glory forever.]'"*

Prayer connects heaven with earth as you come to your Father at His throne, worshipping Him, giving Him your allegiance, and telling Him of your commitment to His will. As you gain heaven's perspective, you lay all earthly matters and concerns at the feet of your sovereign God.

Did you note how the pattern of this prayer changes between verses 10 and 11? The first segment focuses on God and His kingdom, His will. Then in verse 11, having settled these things, you bring the matters of earth to Him, seeking His help: *give, forgive, lead us not, deliver*. Why? Because His is the kingdom, the power, and the glory, forever and ever. Amen! So be it!

God's will is crucial. Desiring it, here, now. Knowing it. Submitting to it.

> **Romans 12:1-2 tells us how to find God's will. Read aloud these verses, printed for you below, before making any observations. It's good to hear Scripture. (I like to listen to it on CDs in the mornings as I get dressed for the day.)**

> 1 *Therefore I urge you, brethren, by the mercies of God, to present your bodies a living and holy sacrifice, acceptable to God, which is your spiritual service of worship.*
> 2 *And do not be conformed to this world, but be transformed by the renewing of your mind, so that you may prove what the will of God is, that which is good and acceptable and perfect.*

"Therefore" follows the statement that "from Him and through Him and to Him are all things. To Him be the glory forever. Amen" (Romans 11:36). Because God is the source, means, and end of all things—and to Him belongs the glory forever—it is our reasonable service of worship to do what Romans 12:1-2 says. The passage calls on us to present ourselves as living sacrifices. Isn't that exactly what we are doing in prayer when we bow before God, hallow His name, pledge our allegiance to His kingdom, and unreservedly submit to His divine will while we live on earth?

How will we know God's will? Read Romans 12:1-2 aloud again. Underline in your Bible every reference to God's will in these verses. Now answer the questions that lead to accurate observation of the text.

- What does the text (especially the parts you've underlined) tell you about God's will? List your insights below.

_____

_____

_____

- What enables you to prove (to put to the test for the purpose of approval) what God's will is?

_____

_____

_____

- According to the text, what would keep you from knowing God's will? What are you *not* to do?

_____

_____

_____

_____

Since God's will is good, acceptable, and perfect, don't you long to be right in the middle of it? Yes, and I want to be right there with you—beside you—knowing without a shadow of doubt that this is the will of God in Christ Jesus concerning me.

I am a lover of Christian biographies, especially those of men and women of past generations. Next to the Word of God, these are the books that helped and encouraged me most as a new Christian, giving me a vision of what it was like to walk with God, believe Him, obey Him, and do His will no matter the cost.

Among these men and women is George Mueller (1806–1898). He was born over two centuries ago, yet his life continues to show that God never changes, that He hears and answers prayer. Until he was converted, Mueller was truly chief among sinners. His conversion came when he saw a group of his contemporaries on their knees in prayer.

But let's allow him to tell his own story of how he came to start his orphanages and, for over 60 years, see God supply the needs of the orphans—sometimes daily, sometimes hourly, without telling anyone of the need but God alone. Let's see what we can learn about prayer and discerning God's will.

> The first and primary object of the Institution was…
> that God might be magnified by the fact that the
> orphans under my care were, and are, provided
> with all they need only by prayer and faith, without
> anyone being asked by me or my fellow-laborers,
> whereby it might be seen that *God is faithful still and
> hears prayer still.*
>
> I never remember in all my Christian course, a
> period now of sixty-nine years and four months, that
> I ever *sincerely and patiently* sought to know the will
> of God by the teaching of the Word of God, but I
> have been *always* directed rightly.
>
> But if honesty of heart and uprightness before

God were lacking, or if I did not patiently wait upon God for instruction, or if I preferred the counsel of my fellow men to the declarations of the Word of the living God, I made great mistakes.[4]

Oh, how well I understand. I have made some very unwise decisions—great mistakes—because I did not wait patiently upon the Lord for instruction. I neglected to diligently seek Him before making a decision. Right now I'm recalling one specific incident where I impulsively "went with my heart" and did what was kind, compassionate, and generous…but not God's will. It was a gift given in a way that violated the Word—and in my rush to help I never thought of the proverb I needed to remember. Years later I reaped the consequences of that decision.

George Mueller applied the following biblical principles in his decision-making. I truly believe they are ones you will want to consider and use. He writes,

1. I seek at the beginning to get my heart into such a state that it has no will of its own in regard to a given matter. Nine-tenths of the difficulties are overcome when our hearts are ready to do the Lord's will, whatever it may be. When one is truly in this state, it is usually but a little way to the knowledge of what His will is.

2. Having done this, I do not leave the result to feeling or simple impression. If so, I make myself liable to great delusions.

3. I seek the will of the Spirit of God through, or in connection with, the Word of God. The Spirit and the Word must be combined. If I look to the Spirit alone without the Word, I lay myself open to great delusions also.

4. Next I take into account providential circumstances. These plainly indicate God's will in connection with His Word and Spirit.

5. I ask God in prayer to reveal His will to me aright.

6. Thus through prayer to God, the study of the Word and reflection, I come to a deliberate judgment according to the best of my ability and knowledge, and if my mind is thus at peace, and continues after two or three petitions, I proceed accordingly. In trivial matters and transactions involving most important issues, I have found this method always effective.[5]

Beloved, aren't you anxious to get on your knees and seek to know God's will?

It's Time to Pray

What do you need to know, to understand? In which areas of your life do you need direction? On a separate piece of paper—or perhaps in a journal or even inside your Bible—write your questions and date them.

Then go to the Father and present yourself as a living sacrifice. Tell Him that His will is your will. You already know it will be "good, acceptable, and perfect," because that's what the will of God is. Spread your list before the Lord and apply what you've learned today. Stay in His Word; it is your book of prayer.

His Mosaic of Exquisite Design

A s you titled each index sentence in the Lord's Prayer, did you find yourself wondering, *But where is intercession? Where is praying for others? I didn't see it in the Lord's Prayer, and surely God wants us to pray for others!*

You are so right. I asked our Father the same question, and when He showed me where it was, I got so excited! Maybe you've already seen it, but in case you haven't, let me show you how to find it. It's the rich fruit of observation.

> **Read through the Lord's Prayer again. Matthew 6:9-13 is printed below.**
>
> • **Mark every singular personal pronoun: *I, me, my, mine.***
>
> • **Mark the plural personal pronouns: *we, our, us.***
>
> • **From memory, write the general topic of each sentence beneath each index sentence. It will be good review.**

"Pray, then, in this way:
'Our Father who is in heaven, hallowed be Your name.

_____

'Your kingdom come.

_____

'Your will be done, on earth as it is in heaven.

_____

'Give us this day our daily bread.

_____

'And forgive us our debts, as we also have forgiven our debtors.

_____

'And do not lead us into temptation, but deliver us from evil.

_____

['For Yours is the kingdom and the power and the glory forever. Amen.']"

_____

What singular personal pronouns did you circle or color?

_____

_____

List the plural personal pronouns you circled or colored.

_____

_____

What does this tell you about intercession?

_____

_____

The "us," "our," and "we" all let us know that prayer is not just about me. It includes others. When you pray "this way," the way Jesus taught us to pray, you are praying for yourself as well as for the body of Jesus Christ. You are also praying for the lost, who have yet to hear and respond to the Great Shepherd (see John 10).

Each index sentence, then, is meant to stimulate not only petition for yourself but also intercession for the body of Jesus Christ. We can appear before the throne of God on behalf of others. What a calling! What a ministry!

Even as I write these words, I have asked my husband, one of my sons, my daughter-in-love (law), our staff, and our leaders to pray for me and this work God has called me to do. I feel so unworthy and inadequate as I realize I have so much to learn about the practice of prayer.

THE MOSAIC OF INTERCESSION

Archaeologists delight in uncovering ancient mosaics, the handiwork of artisans of the past. That's what I want us to do today, Beloved—only the mosaic of intercession we will uncover together will be one of exquisite design, laid out by the master of artisans, God Himself. And wonder of wonders, you will find _yourself_ there, right in His mosaic!

We uncover the first precious stone of truth when we discover that _pray_ and _prayed_ are used for the first time in Genesis 20.

The word "prayed" in Genesis 20:17 can also be translated _intercede_. "Abraham prayed to God, and God healed Abimelech and his wife and his maids, so that they bore children." The word "prayed" is the Hebrew _palal_, which means "to intervene, interpose, pray." At least a dozen Hebrew words exist for pray and prayer. The most common word for prayer, however, is *tepillâ* and the related verb, *palal*. Both the verb and the noun most frequently refer to intercessory prayer.

The context of the first appearance of this word shows one man, Abraham, interceding before God on behalf of Abimelech. A local chieftain in the area, Abimelech took Abraham's wife, Sarah, to his tent, not realizing she was a married woman. The result of Abraham's intercession was healing for Abimelech and Abimelech's wife, whom God had struck with barrenness.

What I want you to see here is that the components connected with the first use of *palal* are sin, intercession, and healing. Healing because of the intercession!

The second precious stone is in Exodus, where God instructed Aaron and his sons as to what they were to wear when they appeared in His presence.

Read Exodus 28:1-6,9-12,15-22,29-30 in your Bible. As you read, look at these drawings from *The New Inductive Study Bible* so you have a visual aid for what is being described.

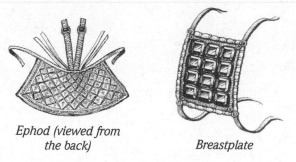

Ephod (viewed from the back)

Breastplate

Draw a red heart over every reference to heart. I do this in my Bible because the heart is so important to God, and is so often referred to. I don't want to miss what God wants me to know.

Stop and think about the *why* of it all. What is the picture God gave to the priests and the people? Can you see any parallel to intercession? Where?

_____

_____

_____

Did you know that Isaiah 53 is one the clearest Old Testament prophecies about the Messiah, the Christ? Look at what Isaiah told us prophetically about Jesus in Isaiah 53:12. Take note of what He did and for whom He intercedes, and write your observation below.

_____

_____

_____

Let's uncover more. Read Isaiah 59:15-16. Note the situation...and then what displeases the Lord.

_____

_____

Does the situation described in Isaiah 59 sound similar to today? To our culture? What was needed?

_____

_____

What did He bring and how?

_____

_____

Let's move to the New Testament and behold the beauty of our Father's mosaic of intercession. The New Testament word for intercession is *huperentugchán*. That's quite a word, isn't it? It comes from two words: from *hupér* which means "for or on behalf of," and *entugchán*, which means "to turn to, appeal, to intercede for or in the behalf of someone, to plead for someone."

> **Look at what God tells us about Jesus Christ. Read Hebrews 4:14 and write what this verse tells you about Him.**

_____

_____

_____

As priests served under the Law, the Old Covenant, so we have a great high priest under the New Covenant—our Lord Jesus Christ. He is the priest who can sympathize with our weaknesses yet who is without sin (see Hebrews 2:14-18; 4:15), One who has appeared in the presence of God for us (9:24). Hallelujah!

> **What is His ministry? Write Hebrews 7:25 below. It's beautiful.**

_____

_____

_____

Are you asking, "Is this where I fit in?" Yes, Beloved, because Jesus continuously intercedes for you before the Father. But there is even more!

Read Revelation 1:5-6 in your Bible. What do you see in these verses that places you in this beautiful mosaic of intercession?

_____

_____

_____

Now add Revelation 5:9-10 to your reading on intercession. From where did those who have been made a kingdom and priests to our God come?

_____

_____

_____

How do you think they came to this status? Do you think it had to do with the intercessory prayers of another child of God, another priest of God who took their calling seriously and interceded for their salvation? Who (and I am speaking figuratively now) interceded for you when you, like Abimelech, needed healing?

Beloved, do you see your high calling? Your ministry is to intercede in prayer for others who, though in a variety of situations, need the touch of God in their lives. We'll see this as we continue looking at what Jesus taught about prayer.

As I share all these things, do you find yourself wanting to say something like this? "But Kay, sometimes I feel so inadequate, so filled with my weaknesses that I don't know how to pray. Sometimes all I can do is groan." Oh Beloved, could the groaning be the Spirit of God within you?

> Read Romans 8:26-27. Put a cloud around every reference to the Spirit and underline every reference to "our," "we," and "us." Put a triangle over every reference to God. Watch the pronouns carefully, and match them with the right noun.

> 26 *In the same way the Spirit also helps our weakness; for we do not know how to pray as we should, but the Spirit Himself intercedes for us with groanings too deep for words;*
> 27 *and He who searches the hearts knows what the mind of the Spirit is, because He intercedes for the saints according to the will of God.*

Faithful one, list what you learn about each one you marked. Let me get you started.

Us	The Spirit	God
we are weak	helps our weakness	

Awesome, isn't it! Jesus Christ intercedes from heaven for you. The Holy Spirit intercedes *in* you. You in turn, as a priest unto God, have the privilege of praying for and interceding for others—the lost and the saved.

You can do kingdom work all around the world on your knees in your closet alone, or gathered with the congregation of fellow believers, members of the church, the body of Jesus Christ of which He is the head.

Can you really comprehend all that God does with your prayers, precious one? Do you realize how important they are to Him? To His kingdom? He keeps them before His throne (Revelation 8:3-5)!

It's Time to Pray

Why don't you sit quietly before the Lord and ask Him to lay a specific person on your heart and mind? Ask God how to pray for this person, to lead you in prayer on his or her behalf.

If you don't know where to begin, try "walking" her or him through prayer by using the pattern of the Lord's Prayer. Begin by either thanking God for _____'s salvation or by praying for it so _____ can truly pray, "Our Father."

Next pray that he or she would hallow His name, give Him total allegiance, and so forth. Have a blessed time interceding, dear one.

A Faith That Soars

G *ive us this day our daily bread."*
Before we look at this fourth index sentence dealing with petition, asking God to provide, let me ask you a question. Have you ever been embarrassed or even afraid to pray for specific things for fear God wouldn't answer your prayer?

I have.

I have thought, *Father, what if You don't answer this prayer? It will leave me hanging! It will look as if prayer doesn't work!* At this point some of you may be laughing at me. I don't blame you, because I'm laughing too! I can hear you saying, "Kay, why put the blame on God if the prayer isn't answered? Why not put it on yourself?"

I'll tell you why! When I pray, I declare my faith in His character and His ways. Then, if it seems as though God didn't come through, it looks as if *He* has failed—not me! Let me give you an illustration from when I was about three or four years old in the Lord. (As the years have gone by, I have come to trust my Father more and to relax in His ways.)

Jack and I were missionaries in Mexico and had taken a group of English-speaking teens on a weekend retreat. Conditions were primitive, but the girls had the best end of the deal. We had an army surplus tent over our heads.

That night as we sat around the campfire and I taught, God really spoke. Several missionary kids who thought they were saved came to the Lord that evening. I am wary of emotional decisions around campfires, so I didn't offer an invitation. Even so, from out of the dark they came, separately, many in tears, telling me they had turned to God and were willing to follow Him totally. God had moved! And time has proven the reality of those commitments.

Well, you can imagine the joy in the tent that night. You know how girls are! They were at fever pitch when all of a sudden we heard a loud, agonized, "Oh, no! I've dropped my contact lens! My parents will *kill* me!"

Now, you know missionary parents are not allowed to kill their children; it's a bad testimony! Gail, however, was rather wild, and had been kicked out of several Christian schools. So she may have been right—it might have crossed her parents' minds!

Contacts weren't disposable in those days, and they were expensive. This was a brand-new one she had gotten to replace another one she had just lost! Replacing contacts is hard on missionary support funds!

Just that quickly, we were all down on our knees with lanterns held above our heads as we looked in green grass for a green-tinted contact. As I crawled in the grass, God reminded me that I had just been teaching these teens about His attributes and His ways.

Ask Me to find it, came the thought. *Ask Me in front of the girls.*

But Father, I prayed silently, *what if I ask You and we don't find it? How will that look?*

I went back to my groping, but I couldn't help thinking, *He does know where it is because He is omniscient, all-knowing. There isn't a thing hidden from His sight.*

Still I resisted. It was just too risky. We might not find it, and then how would God look? I didn't want to risk His reputation in front of ones so young in the faith. (Can you understand what I was going through?)

Well, God won. I called the search to a temporary halt, and there on my knees I prayed aloud. As I did, I fervently reminded God of every promise I could think of that related to our plight. It was not a short prayer, as my faith really needed biblical fuel!

After I finished, we continued to search for a while to the mournful, intermittent tune of Gail's swan song, "My parents are gonna kill me! My parents are gonna kill me!"

When I was almost ready to tell God I never should have prayed aloud, Lily let out a hysterical yelp, "I found it! I found it!" Tears poured down her face. But why? These weren't gushy, sentimental, girlish tears.

I didn't have to wait long to find out. Of all the teens, none was more exemplary in behavior or zeal for missions than Lily. Any one of us would have willingly claimed her as our own because she would have made us look like ideal missionary parents. Lily claimed to have been saved at a very young age, and her behavior gave us no cause to doubt the reality of her profession. She was the opposite of dear Gail! Yet here was that precious girl, tears streaming down her face, half laughing and half crying as she told us her story.

After the lesson around the campfire, Lily realized she really had never been saved. It was hard for her to believe, since she had led so many others to Christ. Yet she knew it was true, so there in the dark the transaction had taken place. Lily passed from death to life, from the power of Satan to the kingdom of God. She received forgiveness of sins and inheritance among those who are sanctified (see Acts 26:18). She had been coming into the tent to tell us, when Gail went into hysterics over her contact.

While I was on my knees looking for the contact and wrestling with God about praying aloud, Lily was praying, *God, You have never directly answered my prayers all these years. Now that I am Yours, prove it by answering this prayer. Let me find Gail's contact.*

Oh, what a precious Father we have! God orchestrated it all by His Spirit because it delighted His Father's heart to confirm her salvation in an answer to very specific prayer.

"Give us this day our daily bread" is a very specific request and prayer that demonstrates our faith. In the light of that experience and in preparation for our study of what it means to ask for daily bread, let me share some truths about faith that I believe will be helpful. We touched on faith at the beginning of our study, but now it's time to go deeper because we have come to the issue of specific prayer.

Hebrews 11 is called the "Faith Chapter." If you were to color every occurrence of faith in its 40 verses, you would readily understand why.

Read Hebrews 11:1-3 in your Bible, then copy Hebrews 11:1 below. As you write it, I want you to do it in a structured way. Also as you write it, say it aloud. You need to hear the words.

Now _____ ____ _____ _____

_____ _____ _____ for, the

_____ ____ _____ _____ seen.

Read Hebrews 11:2. In one word, how did men gain approval?

_____

According to verse 3, how were the worlds prepared? How do you know? Were you there?

_____

_____

_____

_____

How does anyone know the truth of Hebrews 11:3?

_____

_____

Over and over again you will find God reminding His people that He is the Creator of the heavens and the earth. It is one of the fundamentals of a biblical worldview and a matter you need to settle that is determined only by faith. Either you believe God or you believe a theory of man, some claim of science. Whom will you believe?

Believe me, your faith will never truly soar until you believe God.

What is faith? The Greek word for *faith* is *pistis*—a firm persuasion, a conviction based upon hearing. *Pistis* is related to the Greek term *peitho,* or *persuade.* Faith is simply taking God at His Word. It's believing that the Bible is the Word of God.

True faith, not head knowledge, is a firm conviction that brings personal surrender to God and His Word. In turn, our personal surrender will be demonstrated by our daily conduct, in the way we live. James made it clear that our works show forth the reality of our faith. True faith has evidence. The apostle John states the same thing in his first letter. You could easily see it if you were to mark every reference to "know" in 1 John and then look at what God says you know and how you know it. (This is not an assignment, just a suggestion for the future. I mentioned it earlier in our study, but we have covered so much that it bears repeating.)

If God by His word prepared and created the world, can He not by His same powerful Word take care of what He created? Of course He can. We need to say with Jeremiah the prophet, "Ah Lord GOD! Behold, You have made the heavens and the earth by Your great power and by Your outstretched arm! Nothing is too difficult for You" (Jeremiah 32:17) and then hear God respond, "Behold, I am the LORD, the God of all flesh; is anything too difficult for Me?" (verse 27).

In telling us to pray for our daily bread—or "tomorrow's bread," as some interpret it—Jesus reminds us to live out our day-by-day lives in total dependence on God. And faith says, "Amen! He is able!"

Remember what you saw when you did your weekender on Matthew 6? In Matthew 6:25-34 Jesus expanded on this life of total dependence by instructing us, "Do not worry then, saying, 'What will we eat?' or 'What will we drink?' or 'What will we wear for clothing?' For the Gentiles eagerly seek all these things; for your heavenly Father knows that you need all these things."

He knows, Beloved.

He knows, and He is able to supply all your needs according to His riches in Christ Jesus our Lord (Philippians 4:19). You are an heir of God, a joint heir with Jesus Christ. You belong to God.

Pause and think that through: You belong to God. Jesus said,

> Ask, and it will be given to you...If you then, being evil, know how to give good gifts to your children, how much more will your Father who is in heaven give what is good to those who ask Him! (Matthew 7:7,11).

Is your heart burning with desire for God—for pleasing Him with your faith? Mine is. I pray, *Oh Father, I long to live this way. I long to remember. Remind me, remind me. It is so very simple. You say it and I am to believe it. And when I do, I bring You pleasure. Oh God, I want to bring You pleasure.*

It's Time to Pray

Father, is it really time to pray? I'm not so sure. I think it might be time to be still for a while, to sit in Your presence, and to think about living for Your pleasure. Living by faith. For without faith it is impossible to please You. I must believe You are God, a rewarder of those who seek You; and I must live accordingly.

Total Dependence on God

Prayer is a demonstration of your total dependence on God. It makes sense, then, that a major precept of prayer is *asking.*

You may not like that. You may think you ought to be man or woman enough to get what you need on your own. But, dear child of God, if this is what you think, let me gently tell you that you are wrong. To try to meet the needs of soul, body, spirit, or mind apart from seeking Him is to miss some of the riches of His glory that could be yours.

> **Read James 4:1-3 in your Bible. Circle every occurrence of "you" and mark "ask" in the same way have been marking "prayer." Then answer these questions.**
>
> • **What's the conflict? How is it described?**
>
> _____
>
> _____
>
> _____
>
> _____
>
> • **Why does the conflict exist?**
>
> _____
>
> _____
>
> _____

- Why are they asking and not receiving?

_____

_____

_____

_____

- Do you know anyone like this? What is that person's life like?

_____

_____

_____

_____

- Now read James 4:4. What's the problem?

_____

_____

_____

To keep trying to meet your own needs...

- apart from seeking God will end in internal war. Riddled with lust and envy, the desire to satisfy your pleasures causes "war" within (verses 1-3).

- apart from trusting in God will end in quarrels and conflicts (verse 1).

- independently of God is to deny your need of Him (Philippians 4:19).

To go to others for help instead of going to your Father is to live a life of woe:

> Woe to those who go down to Egypt [where you once were in bondage] for help and rely on horses, and trust in chariots because they are many and in horsemen because they are very strong, but they do not look to the Holy One of Israel, nor seek the LORD! (Isaiah 31:1).

To rely on yourself is to live in a stony wilderness:

> Thus says the LORD, "Cursed is the man who trusts in mankind and makes flesh his strength, and whose heart turns away from the LORD. For he will be like a bush in the desert and will not see when prosperity comes, but will live in stony wastes in the wilderness, a land of salt without inhabitant" (Jeremiah 17:5-6).

To live in total dependence on God, however, is to bask in great blessing:

> Blessed is the man who trusts in the LORD and whose trust is the LORD. For he will be like a tree planted by the water, that extends its roots by a stream and will not fear when the heat comes; but its leaves will be green, and it will not be anxious in a year of drought nor cease to yield fruit (Jeremiah 17:7-8).

Why, oh, why will we not humble ourselves, rid ourselves of pride, and realize that apart from God we can do *nothing*, not even supply our own needs? I think this is especially hard for a man because you are to be the strong one, the laborer who provides for his own. However, although it seems to go against the male ego, don't let it stop you, dear brother.

"But," you may say, "those who don't know Jesus supply their own needs and they survive!" Yes, they do survive. But how? Gauge the quality of their life. Where's their peace, confidence, pleasure, and assurance? If it's not in God, where is it? And if it's not in God, what will they do when their source is taken away? God is *El Olam*, the everlasting God. Nothing can ever take Him away from us, and He will never leave or forsake us. He is always there, everywhere-present…and only a prayer, a heart cry, away.

> This I know, that God is for me.
> In God whose word I praise,
> In the LORD, whose word I praise,
> In God I have put my trust, I shall not be afraid.
> What can man do to me?
> —Psalm 56:9-11

One of my favorite little books is *On This Day* by Robert J. Morgan. It's a book of 365 amazing and inspiring stories about saints, martyrs, and heroes. I want to share the story "God's Hand-writing" with you, because it will encourage and delight you with the practicality of depending on God.

> Missionaries Dick and Margaret Hillis found themselves caught in China during the Japanese invasion. The couple lived with their two children in the inland town of Shenkiu. The village was tense with fear; every day brought terrifying reports of the Japanese advance. At the worst possible time, Dick developed appendicitis, and he knew his life depended on making the long journey by rickshaw to the hospital. On January 15, 1941, with deep fore-boding, Margaret watched him leave.
>
> Soon the Chinese colonel came with news. The enemy was near and townspeople must evacuate. Margaret shivered, knowing that one-year-old Johnny and two-month-old Margaret Anne would

never survive as refugees. So she stayed put. Early next morning she tore the page from the wall calendar and read the new day's scripture. It was Psalm 56:3—*"What time I am afraid, I will trust in thee."*

The town emptied during the day, and next morning Margaret arose, feeling abandoned. The new verse on the calendar was Psalm 9:10—*"Thou, Lord, hast not forsaken them that seek thee."*

The next morning she arose to distant sounds of gunfire and worried about food for her children. The calendar verse was Genesis 50:21—*"I will nourish you and your little ones."* An old woman suddenly popped in with a pail of steaming goat's milk, and another straggler arrived with a basket of eggs.

Through the day, sounds of warfare grew louder, and during the night Margaret prayed for deliverance. The next morning she tore the page from the calendar to read Psalm 56:9—*"When I cry unto Thee, then shall my enemies turn back."* The battle was looming closer, and Margaret didn't go to bed that night. Invasion seemed imminent. But the next morning, all was quiet. Suddenly, villagers began returning to their homes, and the colonel knocked on her door.

For some reason, he told her, the Japanese had withdrawn their troops. No one could understand it, but the danger had passed. They were safe.

Margaret glanced at her wall calendar and felt she had been reading the handwriting of God.[6]

You and I have the handwriting of God—the words of God—and it is He who tells us to ask for our daily bread, who tells us not to worry about tomorrow, for tomorrow will take care of itself. Each day has troubles of its own.

According to Matthew 6:33, what is your task?

_____

What is His promise (verse 33)?

_____

_____

(If you don't know or remember what "these
things" are, read Matthew 6:25-33.)

Write out Matthew 6:31-34 on several index cards
and put them in strategic places. Every time you
see the cards, read the passage aloud until you've
memorized it.

We are to do our job and let God do His! We will always mess
up when we try to take over for Him. Plus, He'll never tolerate it.
Remember, we cannot please Him if we refuse to believe Him. We
settled that when we read Hebrews 11:6.

It's Time to Pray

It's time to ask God to search your heart and see if there's any
hurtful way—any way of pain—in you because you are not walking
in total dependence on Him. Ask Him to show you any way, place,
area, or arena in which you are trying to do *His* job—trying to be
God. Write down any insights God gives you and then, calling them
exactly what they are, ask Him to forgive you. He promises He will
cleanse you from all unrighteousness (1 John 1:9).

The LORD Who Provides

Praying God's way means to live in total dependence on our Father. We pray without ceasing, because in Him we live and move and have our being. As we noted earlier, asking in prayer pleases God, for it demonstrates our total dependence on Him as our Father.

How then do we ask?

In our final day of study this week I want to make sure you and I understand the *1, 2, 3, 4,* and *5* of it.

1. WE REALLY DO NEED TO ASK

We can't just assume that our needs will be met, or take God's provision for granted.

Every time we come before God, humble ourselves in His presence, and ask Him to meet our needs, it shows that we acknowledge Him as the Source of all things. This is why, I believe, Jesus says, "Give us this day our *daily* bread." It is to be a day-by-day dependence.

So-called "prosperity theology" is a contemporary teaching that grieves my heart. We often hear about the answers to prayers for prosperity, but not the damage done to the faith of listeners who have been swayed by this "name-it-and-claim-it" teaching. As "King's kids," these teachers tell us, Father God wants us to have the very best—and a lot of it. Yet Jesus' instruction to ask for "daily bread" directly contradicts that teaching!

In our society it's difficult to understand what it means to speak of our daily bread. In biblical times however—or even now in many, many places around our world—the concept wasn't difficult to grasp at all.

As a I showered and dressed a few mornings ago, I listened to the book of Deuteronomy on my CD player. I was struck by the fact that in those days, a laborer was to be paid his daily wage before the sun set because it was his daily sustenance. If he wasn't paid, he and his family didn't eat. Immediately, Jesus' instruction on prayer came to mind.

One of my favorite illustrations goes back to the days of communism in Romania before the death of Nicolae Ceausescu in 1989. When I finished reading the story, all I could do was weep and worship my God.

> Christmas was not to be the same this year. Isolated from the rest of the outside world, it was difficult with the seven children to celebrate the birth of Jesus when their stomachs were empty. There were no decorations, no brightly lit candles, no Christmas tree, no cookies, and no beautifully wrapped gifts to exchange. The children were just as hungry today as any other day. Soon, Dad would be telling the children about the Messiah, born in a manger, much like the little hut they lived in.
>
> This father, mother, and their seven children (all under 14) were banished into exile in the far reaches of an uninhabited part of the country. The Communist authorities hated the father because of his convicting preaching. He was nicknamed by the believers "The Golden Word" because of his eloquence. They were forced to move to a little village, inaccessible by car or train. What little food they were given was flown in by helicopter. They lived in a tiny hut with a straw roof, under constant surveillance of the prison guards.
>
> The village was established for those "undesirables" of society, which includes "religious fanatics."

The stinging chill was made worse by the wind whipping snow across the flat barren land, unbroken by hills, and whistling its song through every crack and crevice in the small hut. For two days now the guards had not bothered to bring them any food. They were too busy preparing their own celebration with wine and pork. The children listened intently to their father telling them the story of Jesus as they huddled together around the dim light of the gas lantern on the table. They were so intent, they forgot about their hunger. But when the story was over, one after the other began to cry. Before going to bed that Christmas Eve, the whole family knelt down on the dirt floor and prayed as never before: "Our Father, which art in Heaven…Give us this day our daily bread."

After they finished their prayer and said, "Amen," the children asked their mother and father many questions.

"Do you think God heard our prayer?"

"Of course He did."

"But what if He didn't hear it?"

"That isn't possible," the father replied.

"Do you think He will send us bread?" they asked.

"Yes, I'm sure He will," said the father.

"But when?" they cried.

The parents, heartbroken to see their children crying from hunger, could not answer. The children continued. "Who will He send to bring us bread?"

"He will find someone," said the father reassuringly.

"But what if He doesn't find anyone?"

"Well then," the father paused, "He Himself will

bring it with His own hand. Now close your eyes and go to sleep."

The father blew out the little lantern as darkness descended on them, and the wind whistled to them in their sleep. Suddenly, the still darkness was shattered by a knock on the door!

The father got out of bed and opened the door just a crack to keep the cold from blowing inside. A hand holding a large loaf of bread was stretched toward him. His heart pounding, the father reached out to take the bread, and at the same time opened the door widely to say thank you. But at that very moment, in the twinkling of an eye, the hand was gone, and there was no one there. Bewildered, the father closed the door and turned around. All seven children leaped out of bed and surrounded him.

"Who was it, Dad? Who gave you the bread?"

"Children," he said with a tremble in his voice, "The Lord did not find anyone to send to us with bread, so He Himself came and gave it to us with His own hand."

Nobody could sleep...The children couldn't stop singing about how the Lord had spread a table for them in the wilderness.[7]

2. We are to ask within the boundaries of God's Word

When the Lord teaches us to ask for our "daily bread," I personally think He is referring to whatever I need to sustain me on any given day. As we study the Word of God, we learn to make our requests within the wise and protective boundaries He has set down for us.

By the way, weigh everything you hear and read about prayer

against the whole counsel of God. When Paul was about to depart for Jerusalem, he gathered the elders from Ephesus and reminded them that he had shared "the whole purpose of God" with them. They were to beware because, after his departure, "savage wolves" would come in and seek to lead people astray (Acts 20:25-32).

If anyone suggests you lay aside the Bible when it comes to prayer, a red flag of danger ought to go up immediately. Remember, the Spirit of God never works apart from or contrary to the Word of God.

> **Mark each reference to prayer and record what the verse or passage teaches you about prayer. Or write out what the verse says. Reading it aloud helps, too.**
>
> **Psalm 145:17-19**
>
> _____
>
> _____
>
> _____
>
> _____
>
> **John 14:13-14**
>
> _____
>
> _____
>
> _____
>
> **John 15:7**
>
> _____
>
> _____

John 15:16

_____

_____

I can't resist sharing two more verses from Ephesians (3:20-21). I love these verses and often use them in prayer. As you read them aloud, mark the word "ask" as you marked *prayer* in the previous verses.

> 20 *Now to Him who is able to do far more*
>   *abundantly beyond all that we ask or think,*
>   *according to the power that works within*
>   *us,*
> 21 *to Him be the glory in the church and in*
>   *Christ Jesus to all generations forever and*
>   *ever. Amen.*

When you pray, learn to plead the promises of God. "For as many as are the promises of God, in Him they are yes" (2 Corinthians 1:20). D.L. Moody, the great evangelist used so mightily by God in America and England in the late 1800s, said, "Tarry at a promise and God will meet you there."

Because the Bible is my prayer book, I have prayed Scripture for years; yet this wonderful principle of pleading the promises of God was crystallized for me years ago when I read this account from Armin Gesswein's School of Prayer.

> Early in the ministry I had an experience that completely changed my understanding of prayer. What a transformation! I was called to start churches and had just discovered "prayer meeting truth" in the Acts. So I started a prayer meeting—the first one I ever attended.

In came an elderly Methodist one night. When he prayed, I detected something new. "I have never heard praying like that," I said to myself. It was not only fervency—I had plenty of that. Heaven and earth got together at once when he prayed. There was a strange immediacy about it. The prayer and the answer were not far apart—in fact they were moving along together. He had it "in the bag" so it seemed to me. The Holy Spirit was right there, in action, giving him assurance of the answer even while he was praying! When *I* prayed, God was "way out there," somewhere in the distance, listening. The answer, too, was in the distance, in the by and by.

Eager to learn his secret, I went to see him one day. His name was Ambrose Whaley, and everyone called him "Uncle Am." He was a retired blacksmith—also a Methodist lay preacher. I soon came to the point: "Uncle Am, I would love to pray with you." At once he arose, led me outside across the driveway into a red barn, up a ladder, into a haymow! There, in some old hay, lay two big Bibles—one open. "What is this?" I thought. I prayed first, as I recall it. Poured out my heart, needs, burdens, wishes, aspirations, ambitions to God. Then he prayed—and there was "that difference" again. There, in that hay, on our knees, at the eyeball level, I said, "Uncle Am, what is it?…You have some kind of a secret in praying. Would you mind sharing it with me?"

I was 24, he was 73 (he lived to be 93), and with an eagle-look in his eyes, he said: *"Young man, learn to plead the promises of God!"*

That did it! My praying has never been the same since. That word completely changed my understanding of prayer. It really revolutionized it! I "saw it" as soon as he said it. Saw what? Well— when I prayed there was fervency, ambition, and so on (the Lord does not put a "perfect squelch" on these either). But I lacked *faith*. Prayer is the key to heaven, but faith unlocks the door. *There must be faith*. Where does that come from? From hearing…*the Word of God*. Uncle Am would plead scripture after scripture, reminding Him of promise after promise, pleading these like a lawyer does his case—the Holy Spirit pouring in His assurance of being heard. This man knew the promises "by the bushel."…I soon learned that he was a mighty intercessor…He prayed *through the Bible*. He taught me the secret of intercessory praying. How can I ever thank God enough for leading me to such a prayer warrior!

What happened? With this discovery, God really *gave me a new Bible!* I had not yet learned how to make the Bible *my prayer book*. It gave me a new motivation for Bible study. I began to "dig in!" I would now search the Scriptures…meditate…mark its many promises…memorize, memorize, *memorize!* There are thousands of promises: a promise for every need, burden, problem, situation.

"Young man, learn to plead the promises of God!"[8]

Uncle Am wasn't the only one who pled the promises of God! He had a long line of predecessors. Search the Old Testament, observe the prayers of men and women of God, and you will find them constantly reminding God of His promises to Abraham, Isaac, and Jacob, and to His covenant people Israel.

3. You must ask according to the will of God

You and I must wait on God in prayer to discern if something is His specific will for us, and when He wants it to happen. So often we hear of how God answered the prayers of others, and we assume He will answer ours in the same way and in the same time frame.

But that's not the way it always works, Beloved.

The fact is, God has a specific plan for each of our lives and a specific work for each of us to do. We saw that in Ephesians 2:10 (see page 91), and it comes out also in Jesus' response to Peter in John 21:20-22. This is also supported in Hebrews 11:32-38.

Some believers experienced glorious deliverances from persecution, illness, or pain. Others suffered greatly. *But God was with them all.* They lived by faith, taking God at His Word. When you ask, remember you've said to God, "Your will be done, on earth as it is in heaven."

4. You are to ask until the answer comes

Asking is not a one-time event. You must never despair of persevering; it keeps you in His presence, where you'll experience fullness of joy and pleasures evermore.

Take a moment and read Luke 18:1-8 in your Bible, remembering that parables are told for a reason.

- **What did Jesus say is the purpose of this parable (verse 1)?**

_____

_____

_____

- **Mark the references to prayer. Don't miss the words used to describe persevering prayer in verse 7. Also** mark "heart," and you will see how it relates to persistent prayer. Now what do you learn for yourself in regard to prayer?

_____

_____

_____

_____

When scholars traced down the source of the 1949 Scottish revival, they found two praying women. These women prayed so long and so diligently without seeing anything happen that one of them in her weariness cried out, "God, if You don't send revival, then I'm not going to speak to You again!"

5. FINALLY, REMEMBER THAT WHEN YOU ASK, ASK FOR OTHERS

Jesus' instructions were "give us *our* daily bread." Every church, every ministry, and every believer needs those who will take our needs before the throne of *Jehovah-Jireh*, the Lord who provides.

It's Time to Pray

What are your needs, Beloved? If you don't have any needs, what needs of others come to mind (a friend, a family member, your church, a ministry)? Review these needs in light of the five points we looked at today, and then pray accordingly.

Once again let's talk about the weekend for a moment. The weekend is never just "our time." It is not meant to be a time of leisure from God—rather it should be one of leisure with God. If you are fortunate enough to not have to work on the weekend, or at least not on one of the days of the weekend, do not use it as a day off from spending time with God. Remember, God ordained the Sabbath as day of rest—and devotion to God.

It is in Him that we live and move and have our being. The very breath you breathe is a gift from Him and is meant to be used not only to sustain life, but to sustain communication with God through prayer.

At the beginning of this week we looked at how intercession is embodied in the Lord's prayer through the "our" and the "us." How well this intercession is modeled for us by Jesus even in the most critical of times. In John 17, Jesus is on His way to the garden of Gethsemane, where He will pray so fervently that He will sweat great drops of blood. It is the Eleven—and us—who are on His heart.

For your weekender assignment, read through John 17:1-26 and color-code in your Bible every reference to those for whom Jesus intercedes. The actual intercession begins in 17:9 and continues throughout the rest of Jesus' prayer. Spend the next two days noting all that Jesus prays for the Eleven *and* for you. And then, think about your co-operation with Him in the answering of this prayer. For instance, in John 17:17 Jesus prays you will be sanctified through truth—His Word. Are you spending time in His Word so this can happen?

As you list all Jesus prays for you, think about these insights and thank God the Father for the intercession of His Son, who has prayed for you according to the Father's will.

Week
Four

Staying in the Word

When Our Prayers
Seem to Hit the Ceiling

Can a child of God ignore the will of God for his or her life, walk in rebellion, and continue to experience the blessings of answered prayer?

No, Beloved, that's not possible.

Jesus told us that we are to ask for God's forgiveness when we don't live righteously before Him. Before we look at the Scriptures and see what God says on this critical issue, let me share a story about what happened to one of our leaders when she heard the truths you are about to study. She relates the following:

> Our home had not sold in more than two years of being on the market. Every time someone came close to purchasing it, the deal fell through. A lady rented it, devastated it, stopped paying rent, and moved out, leaving the house in total disarray.
>
> I thought, *Lord, I know I am Your child, but I don't know why I feel as if my prayers are hitting the ceiling.* We had lost over $11,000 on the home and still hadn't sold it. Each month was an increase of loss in our savings. So I bought the book *Lord, Teach Me to Pray in 28 Days* to discover what could be going on with my prayers not being heard.
>
> Soon I discovered through the study that my 14-year addiction (I was 28 years old) to smoking cigarettes was coming between the Lord and me. I smoked just a few cigarettes a day and had ignored the Holy Spirit's convictions in the past. But now I

heard the Lord speak to my heart very clearly about how those nasty cigarettes were coming before Him because I had continued to ignore His desire for me not to smoke. I cried hard that evening, mourning the fact of what I was doing.

I cried also because I knew I had tried several times before to quit, but could not come clean of the addiction. Every time I passed the back porch the habit would call me, especially in the evening. I was afraid I would heed the call. So that night I prayed. I recognized my sin, acknowledging the fact that I could not quit on my own, but that I wanted to—very badly. I did not want anything to come between the Lord and me in our relationship and my prayers to Him.

But the Lord would have to deliver me, so I asked that He help me overcome and be free of the habit. Needless to say, He healed me of this addiction. I have not desired to smoke since that evening, which is amazing to me!

The experience made me realize that God truly is my healer. Within a month of this experience, our house sold. Within the year, my husband and I received a check for $14,000, which covered our losses. God is a good God.

I believe God did this for me to be healed, to learn of Him, to teach me how to pray and how to approach Him when I come to Him in prayer—without rebellion in my life. When we are in the midst of rebellion, we can't casually approach God in prayer thinking He will ignore our sin and bless us anyway.[9]

Now let's consider the fifth index sentence in the Lord's Prayer. It is critical to our relationship with God because the kingdom of God is all about dealing with sin and finding forgiveness. Read it carefully: "Forgive us our debts, as we also have forgiven our debtors." You might want to underline "as we also" and think about why Jesus used that phrase, and what He was teaching.

As you look at these index sentences, you realize there must be a purpose in their order. Nothing God does is ever random. That's why I wondered, *Father, why are sin and forgiveness not dealt with immediately?*

As I thought about this question, it seemed that if I were to confess sin and to seek to forgive my brother before I did anything else in prayer, the cleansing might be superficial. It might make forgiveness of others even more difficult. Why? Because the immediate focus in prayer would be on myself. But when I begin prayer in worship, longing for His kingdom, committing myself to His will, and come to my Father seeking His provision for my needs—then confession of the debt of righteousness I owe Him cannot help but follow!

Let's reason together: How can you and I genuinely worship God, tell Him we desire His will, and ask Him to supply our needs—without being overwhelmed by our own sin and with our need of His favor in forgiveness? Having come to this point and knowing His forgiveness, how can we withhold forgiveness from those who have trespassed against us, especially when their transgressions against us, fellow sinners, are so minuscule in comparison to our transgressions against the holiness of God?

Think about it, Beloved. Stop for a minute and reflect on what you just read. If you read it quickly, maybe you need to read it again. I want you to follow the logic of the order Jesus gave us in prayer.

God cannot overlook sin. The very nature of His being forbids it. God is holy. Absolutely righteous and pure. Totally separate from humanity and therefore separate and separated from sin. And because God is holy, sin must always be dealt with. The history of Israel testifies to it.

If you were to study nothing but the Torah—the first five books of the Bible—you would know that Israel is suffering today because they collectively do not honor God as God; they don't live by His commandments. They are a divided people seeking to serve God and man, and no one can serve two masters. As a result, they reap the harvest of disobedience.

God knew all this would happen. He spelled out the consequences of disobedience (and the restoration to follow) very clearly in Deuteronomy 27–30. Those consequences have and continue to come to pass. Yet be assured that the Holy One of Israel is their redeemer (see Isaiah 41:14). Israel will be disciplined but not forsaken, because the gifts and calling of God are irrevocable (see Romans 11:29).

Israel is our visual aid, a constant reminder that sin must be dealt with. And it is the same for the true child of God. Hebrews 12, the "chastening or disciplining chapter," tells us that whom the Lord loves He disciplines, and He does it so that we might share His holiness (verses 6,10).

Read Hebrews 12:9-11 in your Bible and watch for the word "chastened" (KJV) or "discipline" (NASB). When you finish, write what God's discipline yields and who benefits. This last question, "who benefits" pertains to you and me, so don't miss it.

- The fruit of discipline is…

_____

- Those who benefit from God's discipline are those who…

_____

- Has God ever disciplined you?

_____

The Greek word for discipline is *paideia*. It is the sum total of child training. Obviously, part of our child training is to pray, "forgive us our debts, as we also have forgiven our debtors."

Now then, precious child of God, if you want to see the holiness of God, take a long, careful look at Calvary. Who crucified His only begotten Son on Golgotha's hill of shame? Who let Jesus cry from the bowels of His being, "My God, My God, why have You forsaken Me?" (Matthew 27:46)? Who let Jesus taste death for all (Hebrews 2:9)?

It was the One with eyes too pure to behold iniquity (Psalm 22:1-3; Habakkuk 1:13). It was the One not satisfied with the blood of bulls and goats, which could never take away sin (Hebrews 10:4-8). It was the One who said, "Without shedding of blood there is no forgiveness" (9:22). It was the One whose holiness was satisfied at Calvary when the sinless Lamb of God was slaughtered... the Lamb "who takes away the sin of the world" (John 1:29).

In His holiness, God "made Him [Jesus] who knew no sin to be sin on our behalf, so that we might become the righteousness of God in Him" (2 Corinthians 5:21).

"But Kay," you may reply, "if all my sins were forgiven at Calvary, why do I need to confess them again, asking His forgiveness? Aren't they already forgiven?"

Yes, all sin—past, present, and future—was dealt with at Calvary. "We have been sanctified through the offering of the body of Jesus Christ once for all" (Hebrews 10:10). However, although sin was paid for in full at Calvary, sin unconfessed and unforsaken puts a barrier between God and His child.

> **Listen to the Word of the Lord and mark every reference to prayer and to sin (including synonyms such as "not listening to God's law," "iniquity," and "doing evil"). Put a big "S" over sin, or color it brown. Mark "prayer" as you've been doing. Read each verse carefully, and listen to the heart of God as He speaks of sin.**

> *He who turns away his ear from listening to the law, even his prayer is an abomination (Proverbs 28:9).*

Isaiah 59:1-2:

> 1 *Behold, the LORD's hand is not so short that it cannot save; nor is His ear so dull that it cannot hear.*
>
> 2 *But your iniquities have made a separation between you and your God, and your sins have hidden His face from you so that He does not hear.*

> *If I regard wickedness in my heart, the LORD will not hear (Psalm 66:18).*

> *The eyes of the Lord are toward the righteous, and His ears attend to their prayer, but the face of the Lord is against those who do evil (1 Peter 3:12).*

> *Confess your sins to one another, and pray for one another so that you may be healed. The effective prayer of a righteous man can accomplish much (James 5:16).*

Reason with me. If there is no need to confess our sins because Jesus has paid for them, then why would Jesus include this as an integral part of prayer?

When Jesus said, "Forgive us our debts," He was talking about our moral debts, our sins. We owe God absolute righteousness. To sin is to be in debt! Every time we do not act righteously (do what God says is right), we are in debt to God and must ask forgiveness. We have offended our holy Father.

Write 1 John 1:9 below. As you record it, say the words aloud.

_____

_____

_____

_____

The word translated "confess" is *homologeo*, and it means "to say the same thing." In other words, you name sin for what it is; you call it what God calls it.

It's time to name any sin that needs to be confessed and to ask God to forgive you the debt of righteousness you owe Him. I can tell you with the voice of experience that there is no better feeling in the world than to know you are right with God, at peace with Him.

It's Time to Pray

Read King David's prayer of confession in Psalm 51. Ask God to reveal to you any debt of righteousness you owe Him. Then pay that debt by agreeing with God, confessing your sin.

You might want to take a piece of paper and write down everything God shows you. When you finish, write over it 1 John 1:9, tear up the piece of paper, and throw it away.

You have His Word that He will forgive you and restore you. Proverbs 28:13 says, "He who conceals his transgressions will not prosper, but he who confesses and forsakes them will find compassion." Listen to your Father: "To this one I will look, to him who is humble and contrite of spirit, and who trembles at My word" (Isaiah 66:2).

Forgiveness Is Our Response to God

Book after book has been written on the subject of forgiveness. Have you ever wondered why?

Simply because it can be so difficult—sometimes seemingly impossible—to forgive others for defrauding us, betraying our trust, or deeply wounding us. We can come up with hundreds of reasons not to forgive.

"If I forgive her, she'll get away with the awful thing she did."

"What he did to me was so destructive, it ruined my life."

"He doesn't deserve to be forgiven."

Our reasons for not forgiving seem quite logical—even reasonable.

Nevertheless, His Word still stands. We are to forgive, and the forgiveness we seek from God is in direct correlation to our willingness to forgive others: "Forgive us our debts, as we also have forgiven our debtors."

It is significant that Jesus began a teaching on forgiveness as soon as He finished teaching His disciples about prayer. It's as if He wanted to make certain we understood the necessity to forgive others.

> **Write Matthew 6:14-15 below. As you do, read the words aloud. Note the word "but."**

_____

_____

_____

_____

Now read Ephesians 4:31-32. What parallel do you see between this passage and Matthew 6:12,14-15?

_____

_____

_____

Look at Colossians 3:12-13. This passage on forgiveness gives us another view into what we are forgiving. What is it?

_____

_____

_____

Peter asked Jesus, "How often shall my brother sin against me and I forgive him?" (Matthew 18:21). In Jesus' answer, you will find your answer on the necessity of forgiveness. I've printed Matthew 18:21-35 below so we can observe the same translation and not miss a thing. Underline or color in red all references to *forgive* and *forgave*.

> 21 *Then Peter came and said to Him, "Lord, how often shall my brother sin against me and I forgive him? Up to seven times?"*
> 22 *Jesus said to him, "I do not say to you, up to seven times, but up to seventy times seven.*
> 23 *"For this reason the kingdom of heaven may be compared to a king who wished to settle accounts with his slaves.*
> 24 *"When he had begun to settle them, one who owed him ten thousand talents was brought to him.*

25 "But since he did not have the means to repay, his lord commanded him to be sold, along with his wife and children and all that he had, and repayment to be made.

26 "So the slave fell to the ground and prostrated himself before him, saying, 'Have patience with me and I will repay you everything.'

27 "And the lord of that slave felt compassion and released him and forgave him the debt.

28 "But that slave went out and found one of his fellow slaves who owed him a hundred denarii; and he seized him and began to choke him, saying, 'Pay back what you owe.'

29 "So his fellow slave fell to the ground and began to plead with him, saying, 'Have patience with me and I will repay you.'

30 "But he was unwilling and went and threw him in prison until he should pay back what was owed.

31 "So when his fellow slaves saw what had happened, they were deeply grieved and came and reported to their lord all that had happened.

32 "Then summoning him, his lord said to him, 'You wicked slave, I forgave you all that debt because you pleaded with me.

33 'Should you not also have had mercy on your fellow slave, in the same way that I had mercy on you?'

34 "And his lord, moved with anger, handed him over to the torturers until he should repay all that was owed him.

35 *"My heavenly Father will also do the same to you, if each of you does not forgive his brother from your heart."*

What did you learn from marking the references to forgiving?

_____

_____

_____

_____

- **According to verse 35, what is the bottom line of this story of the king and the two slaves? And who is bottom-lining it?**

_____

_____

_____

- **What is God's word to you?**

_____

- **From what you have seen in God's Word, is there any way to get around forgiveness? (Remember Matthew 6:14-15.)**

_____

_____

Now listen carefully, Beloved. Forgiving someone does not mean you are releasing him or her from God's just punishment. Only God can do that. To obtain forgiveness they must believe on the Lord Jesus Christ, just as we had to do; otherwise, there is no forgiveness of their sins. If they do not believe, they will be judged according to their deeds, all of which are written in the books (Matthew 25:41,46; Revelation 20:11-15).

God will deal justly with all who sin. But that is *God's* business, not yours. Yours is to forgive.

Have you seen, dear one, that forgiving others is a response of faith, an act of obedience? Obedience isn't always easy; even so, we forgive because God tells us to forgive. It may not seem humanly reasonable or even emotionally possible. However, although you cannot rationalize it in your mind or you don't feel a thing, you step out in faith's obedience because that's what God has told you to do.

Dear brother, dear sister, do you understand that forgiveness isn't a matter of feeling or emotion, that it is an act of your will, a matter of faith's obedience? Forgiveness is your response to God, not to your fellow man. Your transgressor may not deserve it, desire it, or require it; yet you forgive because you know that your Father wants you to. Refusing to forgive is nothing less than disobedience to the Lord, and a sin against Him. When you sin and don't repent, you invite the discipline of your heavenly Father, because a holy God must deal with sin.

Unforgiveness is not only sinful, it is also self-destructive. It will cannibalize your soul, eating you up from the inside out. An unwillingness to forgive leads to a root of bitterness that causes trouble and defiles many (Hebrews 12:14-15). When you make the choice to forgive, however—when you send away their debt—you'll find yourself released from the torturers.

Time and space don't permit, but I could tell you story after story of what happened when people were finally willing to forgive. Just remember, we're all in the same boat. *The entire kingdom of God is comprised of people who have been forgiven their sin and reconciled to God.* And it all happened when we were still enemies! God's Word says, "While we were enemies we were reconciled to God" (Romans 5:10).

Do you see it, dear one? Every human being in the kingdom of God is a sinner—has offended a holy God and transgressed against Him. And every one of us has been forgiven by Him and reconciled to Him through believing in the death, burial, and resurrection of Jesus Christ.

Think, Beloved. If a God who never sinned has forgiven us, how can we, as sinners, refuse to forgive one another?

It's Time to Pray

"Forgive us…as we also have forgiven." It's time to ask God if you need to forgive anyone. Does anyone owe you a debt you need to cancel? You've read His words. If you want forgiveness from your heavenly Father, then you must forgive.

Talk to your Father about it, and remember you've already prayed, "Your will be done, on earth as it is in heaven."

On a yellow sticky note or a card you can place in your Bible, list the names of those you need to forgive. Next to each name write, "On this date [and record the date] I chose to forgive you." And then, hear your Father's "Well done. I am so pleased with you."

The Heart of an Intercessor

*R*evival!

It's a familiar word in many church circles. In times past, we've all seen "revival" advertised as an event on signs in front of churches.

Revival is the plea of many a fervent spirit in private and in public prayer, "Oh God, have mercy, send revival." It is a divine moving of God that brings contrition and confession at the price of personal pride.

Revival is a humbling of our souls that causes us to do away with sin and to live righteously in the midst of a crooked and perverse generation. It is an abhorrence of sin and a craving of righteousness. Revival is nothing less than a gracious, sovereign move of God in the midst of a needy people who are beseeching God for His merciful intervention.

The one common denominator of all revivals is the acute awareness of sin and a cry for God's mercy. It is an overwhelming consciousness of the incomparable holiness and purity of God that causes one to agonize over sin. It's a burning desire to confess all transgressions and be right with God, to seek reconciliation that you once refused to consider, to make restitution whatever the cost. Revival begins with the church and then moves to the streets, bringing the worst of reprobates to their knees for salvation.

For the past two days we have dealt with the issue of sin on an individual level—the personal confession of sin and the need to forgive, but we have not yet touched the "us" that Jesus included in the way to pray: "Forgive us our debts, as we also have forgiven our debtors." This index sentence also deals with the *us*, the *our*: the acknowledgment of corporate sin and failure, of transgression and lawlessness, of compromise and complacency toward God and His Word. Recognizing and confessing these sins together can move us into revival as a church.

How desperately we need it! Pollsters tell us that those who profess to believe in the Lord Jesus Christ more closely resemble the world than their Lord. If all members of the body of Christ would allow themselves to be cleansed with the washing of the water of the Word, if everyone would pursue peace with all men and holiness (sanctification) as Hebrews 12:14 says, then there would be no need for corporate revival, and the world would not be shouting "Hypocrite!" They would either hate us or be converted, because they would see an uncompromising love for God.

Sin is contagious, spreading like a deadly virus. The Bible likens sin to leaven that permeates an entire lump of dough. When sin is ignored or swept under the rug in the house of God, it ruins the spiritual health of the church and calls for God's judgment. If we won't judge sin in ourselves, then God must. This, I believe, is why Jesus included the "us" when it comes to asking forgiveness of our sins.

Are you familiar with Paul's words in 1 Corinthians 5:6-8, where he called the church to account for their arrogance in tolerating and refusing to deal with sin in their midst? How could the very ones who had been saved from sin condone or turn a blind eye to sin in the body of Christ?

> Look up 1 Corinthians 5:6-8 in your Bible. I want you to know what side of the page these verses are on so you can find them when you need them. For our purposes, they are printed below. Read the verses again, aloud, and do the following:
>
> • Mark the reference to Passover with a red half-circle like this: ⌒

- Underline each place "leaven" is used, and then list what you observe from the references to leaven in these verses.

_____

_____

_____

_____

1 Corinthians 5:6-8:

   6 *Your boasting is not good. Do you not know that a little leaven leavens the whole lump of dough?*

   7 *Clean out the old leaven so that you may be a new lump, just as you are in fact unleavened. For Christ our Passover also has been sacrificed.*

   8 *Therefore, let us celebrate the feast, not with old leaven, nor with the leaven of malice and wickedness, but with the unleavened bread of sincerity and truth.*

- The reason for getting rid of the leaven is because Christ our Passover has been sacrificed. Why was Christ sacrificed? (See John 1:29.)

_____

_____

_____

- How are we as children of God to celebrate "the feast"? (This is a picture of what Jesus accomplished for us in His death, keeping us from the wages of sin, which is death.)

_____

_____

_____

Are you celebrating the feast, Beloved, by living according to truth rather than the devil's lie? Are you sincere—covering up nothing? I was told that the word *sincere* was inscribed on fine pottery in ancient times to indicate there were no cracks from its firing in the kiln that had been covered by wax. (The cracks could be detected by holding the pottery up to the light of the sun.)

In Ezekiel 9, God was getting ready to send His destroyers in judgment on His rebellious city, Jerusalem. Before doing so, however, He called for a man with a writing case to go through the city and mark the forehead of all those "who sigh and groan over all the abominations which are being committed in its midst" (Ezekiel 9:4).

These are the ones who will be protected when God's rod of judgment falls on a land that "is filled with blood and...perversion" (verse 9). They are the ones who abhor sin and grieve over the condition of God's chosen people. And what of the others? "My eye will have no pity nor will I spare, but I will bring their conduct upon their heads" (verse 10).

It is time, Beloved, to sigh and groan, to let our hearts be broken over the things that break God's heart. So let's look at the aspect of prayer—the "forgive us our sin"—that deals with corporate sin, the collective sin holding sway in the body of Christ. You can examine two different passages, one in Ezra and another in Daniel. Chronologically, Daniel precedes Ezra. Daniel spoke from captivity in Babylon, while Ezra dealt with the remnant who later left Babylon to return to Jerusalem and rebuild the temple.

Choose one of the passages, or if you have time, both: Daniel 9:1-22 or Ezra 9:1-10. As you read, note how God is approached in prayer.

• What is the attitude, the heart, of the intercessor?

_____

_____

_____

• Mark every reference to sin (*iniquity, transgression, wickedness, rebelled, turned aside from Your commandments*). Don't miss a synonym or any specified sin mentioned in Ezra. (If you choose to study Ezra, please check out Deuteronomy 7:1-6.)

• List what you learn from marking the references to sin.

_____

_____

_____

_____

• What happened as a result of the intercession?

_____

_____

_____

• In light of what you have learned today about intercession, what can you apply to your own prayer life?

Write it down…and with God's help, begin to put
it into practice.

_____

_____

It's Time to Pray

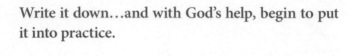

Sit quietly before the Lord and reflect on the condition of the church
to which you belong, and on Christianity in general in our nation.
How do we fall short of God's standard of righteousness? What are
our "collective" or "corporate" sins? Certainly, materialism is one and
immorality is another. What about being too busy to study God's
Word and, as a result, unable to handle the challenges we face?

Write down what comes to mind and keep the list in your Bible.
Add to it as God continues to show you the condition of the church
and a nation that once honored Him.

Then step into the roles of Daniel and Ezra, interceding for the
people in your life as they interceded for the people in theirs.

- Begin by acknowledging the character and righteousness of God and His desire for His people to "be
  holy even as I am holy."

- Confess the sins of the people. Let your heart be
  broken with the things that break God's heart. If you
  studied the Daniel passage, you saw Daniel include
  himself as he confessed the shortcomings of Israel.

- Ask God to show you how to plead with Him on
  behalf of His people. Ask Him to move by His Spirit
  upon the hearts of people, to revive them, and to be
  merciful and compassionate to them.

Guard Duty for the Body

How I will miss studying His Word with you! I know, Beloved, that if you have done your homework, if you have given yourself to the disciplined study of His Word with a heart to hear and obey truth, that God has done a wonderful work within you. I also know that if you will continue to discipline yourself to discover truth for yourself and live in the light of it, God will bring you to an even greater maturity and usefulness in His kingdom.

That usefulness in His kingdom will be realized in part as you pray according to the sixth index, or topical sentence, of prayer: "And do not lead us into temptation, but deliver us from evil."

The final phrase could also be translated *"from the evil one."*

The evil one is the devil, Satan, the prince of this world and of the power of the air, the murderer, the liar and father of lies, the one who does not abide in truth, the tempter, the deceiver, the accuser of the brethren who reigns over evil, the destroyer.

Jesus' use of plural pronouns as He taught us to "pray in this way" underlines the fact that the Lord's Prayer is not just "all about me." When you and I believe on the Lord Jesus Christ and become children of God, we are placed into the body of Christ. As Ephesians teaches, we become part of the church, where the proper function of every member is critical to the health of His body.

If I choose to sin, my disobedience does not affect just me alone!

The devil would love to deceive us on this point, convincing us, "I'll only be hurting myself." But that's not true. Disease in one part of the body affects the whole body. That's why asking God to "lead us not into temptation but deliver us from evil" is so crucial.

This is where we exercise vigilance.

This is where God puts us on guard duty.

Some people express problems with the fact that we would even have to say to God, "Do not lead us into temptation." After all, James 1:13-14 teaches, "Let no one say when he is tempted, 'I am being tempted by God'; for God cannot be tempted by evil, and He Himself does not tempt anyone. But each one is tempted when he is carried away and enticed by his own lust."

So what are we to conclude here? Since Scripture cannot contradict Scripture, one thing is obvious: We aren't pleading with God not to tempt us. We aren't asking Him to refrain from soliciting us to do evil. The fact is, God cannot act in unrighteousness. So what is this portion of the prayer saying?

Let me go into a little detail that I believe will give you the answer you're looking for. As I do, stick with me, because I need to get technical. It's okay to be stretched!

- "Lead," in the Greek, is *eispher,* which means "to bring to." It is an *aorist active subjunctive* verb.

- The *aorist tense* denotes *punctiliar* action, occurring at one particular time.

- The *active voice* indicates that the subject produces the action of the verb. Therefore, it is God who brings or does not bring us into temptation.

- The *subjunctive mood* is a mood of probability and expresses an action that may or should happen but that's not necessarily true at present.

So what do we conclude here? The statement, "Do not lead us into temptation," is saying, in essence, *"God, I am asking You not to bring us into temptation at any point in time."*

Now, before you lean back in unbelief that God would ever bring us "into temptation," let's look at the word translated *temptation.* Then we will put it together in a practical way. The Greek word is *peirasmos,* and is used for trials of varied character: trials, testings, temptations. This word *peirasmos,* then, must be interpreted according to its context. For instance, in James 1:2,12 *peirasmos* describes a trial we are to rejoice in, while in James 1:13-14 the same root word is used in connection with sin and is a temptation to be avoided.

What then is Matthew 6:13 saying? Well, we know it is *not* saying, "God, don't lead me into sin," because that's contrary to His character. What then is Jesus calling us to cover in prayer?

I believe this index sentence is a reminder or a call to vigilance in "preventive" prayer. When you come to this final topic of prayer, you are letting God know that your heart is set on righteousness, that you do not want to fall or to fail. When you find yourself in a trial (*peirasmos*), if you do not count it all joy (James 1:2), you are often tempted to give way to your flesh. If you do not realize that "the testing of your faith produces endurance" and you do not "let endurance have its perfect result, so that you may be perfect and complete, lacking in nothing" (James 1:3-4), then you are liable to respond improperly in that trial, fall prey to the evil one, and yield to temptation.

Let me give you a very ordinary illustration to which we all can relate. Jack and I had to be in Atlanta for a 12:30 PM appointment. Because this involves a two-hour trip, we had to leave Chattanooga at 10:30 AM. At 10:25 Jack walked out the door to go to the office, which is on the grounds where we live. Panicking, I ran after him to tell him we had to leave in five minutes.

At 10:35 I poured my sweet husband some coffee for the trip.

At 10:45 I called the office in desperation, only to find that *he had gone to the bank.*

To put it bluntly, I was flat-out angry. The coffee was cold, and so was I! By 11:00 I was so angry I could have cried. I had so carefully planned my morning for an on-time getaway, and now my plans were going up in smoke. There was no way we could make our appointment on time. In Jack's absence, I sat and tried to read a book on prayer, but concentration was impossible.

At 11:05 I heard a horn honk. As I walked out the door, mouth firmly set in displeasure, James 1:2-3 suddenly leaped into my mind: "Consider it all joy...trials...produces endurance." I got in the car, started to be ugly, but decided instead to walk by the Spirit and not fulfill the desire of my flesh. Our trip was sweet only because I decided in my trial, my *peirasmos,* to rein in my flesh by yielding to the Spirit, whose fruit is love, joy, peace, and self-control! (Which of you was praying for me on that day? How I appreciate it!)

Can you begin to see how this index sentence on deliverance works? "Do not lead us into temptation, but deliver us from evil." We are telling God we do not want to be caught in the devil's snare. This is preventive prayer, solicited and heard by our Father. And who do you think brought that Scripture to my mind as I walked out the door?

Let me give you another outstanding and helpful passage that parallels this index sentence on deliverance: Matthew 26:36-46. Let's return to the garden of Gethsemane. Read this passage carefully and then answer the questions that follow. Don't be tempted and go any further until you do this, Beloved. Don't miss the joy of discovering truth for yourself!

> **As you read from your Bible, note or mark any references to "watching" and "praying."**
>
> • **What is the cup Jesus wanted His Father to remove? Compare this with John 18:11 and record your answer.**
>
> _____
>
> _____
>
> • **What do you learn from noting or marking the references to "watching" and "praying"?**
>
> _____
>
> _____

- List any parallel(s) between this prayer and the Lord's Prayer.

_____

_____

_____

_____

_____

To me, Matthew 26:41, "Keep watching and praying that you may not enter into temptation," is almost an exact reiteration of what we are to pray in the Lord's Prayer. It is an acknowledgment that our flesh is weak even though our spirit is willing. It is an awareness of our utter dependence on God and our utter impotence against temptation apart from Him. Even Jesus asked three of His·disciples to "keep watch with Him" (verses 38,40).

And what happened to Peter? He slept.

Why did he fall asleep? Because he didn't watch and pray!

As a result, he ended up denying his Lord. This was the very fact Peter would write about in his later years: that his adversary, the devil, was prowling about as a roaring lion seeking someone to devour (1 Peter 5:8). Jesus had already told Peter that Satan desired to sift him as wheat and that He had prayed for him (Luke 22:31-32). And yet, despite the Lord's clear warning, Peter was not vigilant. Ultimately, Peter won the battle; his faith did not fail. He was not rendered impotent after his denial, but was used of God to strengthen the brethren. (But as verse 62 tells us, he was not spared from sorrow, regret, and bitter weeping.)

This final petition for deliverance in the Lord's instructions about the way to pray is an acknowledgment of the reality of spiritual warfare.[10] Aware that Satan desires to sift us as wheat, even as he did Peter (verse 31), we are telling God we realize that we cannot handle the evil one alone. We are willing to stand in righteousness, but God must do the delivering.

Oh, how you and I need to see this truth! Deliverance is always available for those who truly want it. Jesus will not have us pray a prayer that God will not answer! No Christian can ever say, "The devil made me do it!" We have the promise of 1 Corinthians 10:13:

> No temptation [*peirasmos*] has overtaken you but
> such as is common to man; and God is faithful, who
> will not allow you to be tempted beyond what you
> are able, but with the temptation will provide the way
> of escape also, so that you will be able to endure it.

Our final prayer is a prayer for deliverance. It is a cry to God out of poverty of spirit (Matthew 5:3), out of grief for falling short of His standard of holiness (5:4), out of meekness (5:5), out of a hunger and thirst for righteousness (5:6), and out of purity of heart (5:8). It is a cry that prays, "Spare me, Father, from needless trials or testings, in which I might find myself tempted." Its cry acknowledges the reality of the evil one and the Christian's warfare. It acknowledges that the flesh is weak. And last but not least, it heeds our Lord's admonition to "keep watching and praying that you may not enter into temptation" (Matthew 26:41).

It's Time to Pray

Today I want us to focus on ourselves. Like the flight attendant says when giving instructions for takeoff, put the oxygen mask on yourself first so you can help those who need your assistance. You and I need to be kept from temptation so we will be on "praying ground," as the saying goes, and can intercede for others—a subject we will talk more about tomorrow.

Sit quietly before the Lord and ask Him to remind you of areas in which you are most vulnerable. Turn each of these areas into a matter of prayer. Ask God to deliver you from situations in which you might be tempted. Verbally affirm your hunger and thirst for righteousness, your desire for purity of heart.

Tell God you want to "be of sober spirit, be on the alert" for you know "your adversary, the devil, prowls around like a roaring lion, seeking someone to devour" and you want "to resist him, firm in your faith" (1 Peter 5:8-9).

When you finish, thank God for hearing your prayer. Remember His promise that if we abide in Him and His words abide in us, we can ask whatever we wish and it will be done (John 15:7).

Our Hallelujah of Worship

We are to resist the devil and remain firm in our faith. One way we can do so is through prayer—vigilant, preventive prayer for ourselves and our brothers and sisters in Christ. Their welfare, their steadfast endurance, impacts the entire body of Jesus Christ. What a high calling we have in this arena of prayer.

As I write this, I think of a missionary in Africa who awoke to find a strange man at the foot of her bed. His intention clearly was to assault her. Although frightened, a calmness came over her, and her first impulse was to ask God what to do. She felt she was to show no fear but to rebuke him and command him to leave, which she did. Shocked, the man looked at her and fled.

Not too long after that, the missionary received a letter from one of her supporters telling her she had been awakened in the night to pray for her protection and wisdom. Immediately the intercessor went to her knees and stayed there until she had peace. She had stood guard in prayer, and the missionary had been delivered from the evil one. When the missionary looked at the time of her intercessor's prayer, she realized that her protector in prayer had been on her knees before and during the man's appearance at the foot of her bed.

Such events happen over and over again. It's part of the mystery of the power of prayer—and you and I, Beloved, can be part of these wonderful tales of deliverance if we will stand guard in prayer as faithful intercessors.

Let's look now at some references to prayer and to deliverance in the Word of God so we can see practically how all this works. It will not only bless you—it will also equip you to give yourself to prayer.

Paul knew the power of vigilance in prayer. Read the following passages and...

- Mark any references to prayer as you've done previously.
- Note what is being requested and underline it.
- Circle the reason for the request if it is stated.
- Write any personal insight or truth you want to remember.
- If you have time, mark the same references in your Bible.

Romans 15:30-32:
> 30 Now I urge you, brethren, by our Lord Jesus Christ and by the love of the Spirit, to strive together with me in your prayers to God for me,
> 31 that I may be rescued from those who are disobedient in Judea, and that my service for Jerusalem may prove acceptable to the saints;
> 32 so that I may come to you in joy by the will of God and find refreshing rest in your company.

2 Corinthians 1:8-11:
> 8 We do not want you to be unaware, brethren, of our affliction which came to us in Asia, that we were burdened excessively, beyond our strength, so that we despaired even of life;
> 9 indeed, we had the sentence of death within ourselves so that we would not trust in ourselves, but in God who raises the dead;

10 who delivered us from so great a peril of
death, and will deliver us, He on whom we
have set our hope. And He will yet deliver
us,

11 you also joining in helping us through your
prayers, so that thanks may be given by
many persons on our behalf for the favor
bestowed on us through the prayers of
many.

Ephesians 6:18-20:

18 With all prayer and petition pray at all
times in the Spirit, and with this in view, be
on the alert with all perseverance and petition for all the saints,

19 and pray on my behalf, that utterance may
be given to me in the opening of my mouth,
to make known with boldness the mystery
of the gospel,

20 for which I am an ambassador in chains;
that in proclaiming it I may speak boldly,
as I ought to speak.

Philippians 1:15-20:

15 Some, to be sure, are preaching Christ even
from envy and strife, but some also from
good will;

16 the latter do it out of love, knowing that I
am appointed for the defense of the gospel;

17 the former proclaim Christ out of selfish
ambition rather than from pure motives,
thinking to cause me distress in my impris-
onment.

18 What then? Only that in every way,

whether in pretense or in truth, Christ is
proclaimed; and in this I rejoice. Yes, and I
will rejoice,

19 for I know that this will turn out for my
deliverance through your prayers and the
provision of the Spirit of Jesus Christ,

20 according to my earnest expectation and
hope, that I will not be put to shame in
anything, but that with all boldness, Christ
will even now, as always, be exalted in my
body, whether by life or by death.

2 Thessalonians 3:1-3:

1 Finally, brethren, pray for us that the word
of the Lord will spread rapidly and be glorified, just as it did also with you;

2 and that we will be rescued from perverse
and evil men; for not all have faith.

3 But the Lord is faithful, and He will
strengthen and protect you from the evil one.

Now consider what Paul urged us to pray for in these verses, and
think of how this would fit in the category of vigilance—deliverance
from evil. As you do, think of what you hear and read in the news
about attacks against Christianity around the world—and even in
our own nation.

First of all, then, I urge that entreaties and prayers,
petitions and thanksgivings, be made on behalf of all
men, for kings and all who are in authority, so that
we may lead a tranquil and quiet life in all godliness
and dignity. This is good and acceptable in the sight
of God our Savior, who desires all men to be saved
and to come to the knowledge of the truth (1 Timothy 2:1-4).

Precept Ministries International works in 150 countries and in 70 languages through the nationals we have trained in these nations. They are people of dedication and great passion, absolutely convinced that each person, young or old, should know how to "discover truth for yourself." Each has counted all things as loss so that others might know their God through studying His Word inductively. In order to accomplish this, many lay their freedom and their lives on the line day after day.

Sometimes I am overwhelmed by their circumstances and by their sacrifice. I think, *What can I do? How can I help?* It doesn't seem like much to say, "I can pray," until I do a study like this and see the importance of vigilance in praying for the deliverance of my brothers and sisters, and for the authorities over those countries. Then I begin to comprehend the vital, critical, protective role and power you and I have in prayer.

To pray this way is to pray our way to victory, for this aspect of prayer says, "I know that we—my brothers and sisters and I—are engaged in warfare, and we will to persevere, to be faithful unto death. We choose to win—and win we shall with the help of each others' prayers and the power of the Spirit of God." Surely those who pray this way are "on the alert with all perseverance and petition for all the saints" (Ephesians 6:18), and Jesus our Teacher is pleased.

Although the last sentence of Jesus' instruction in prayer, "For Yours is the kingdom and the power and the glory forever. Amen," is not in the earliest manuscripts, is it any wonder that it was added as a hallelujah of triumph, of worship? It makes the seventh index sentence—and seven is the number of perfection—which gives this prayer a sense of completeness.

Oh, Beloved, pause a minute. Hush! Listen! Can't you hear the hallelujahs from heaven? "Thanks be to God, who always leads us in triumph in Christ" (2 Corinthians 2:14)! Here we have the perfect way to pray, taught to us by the One who ever lives to make intercession for the children of God. We know how to pray, don't we, Beloved! We know what to pray!

> Pray, then, in this way: "Our Father who is in heaven, hallowed be Your name. Your kingdom come. Your will be done, on earth as it is in heaven. Give us this day our daily bread. And forgive us our debts, as we also have forgiven our debtors. And do not lead us into temptation, but deliver us from evil. [For Yours is the kingdom and the power and the glory forever. Amen]" (Matthew 6:9-13).

It's Time to Pray

I don't think anything would be more fitting than to close our study in watching and praying for the body of Christ, by taking the truths we learned these past two days and putting them into practice. For whom can we specifically pray?

Ask your Father to show you those He wants you to intercede for today, that they would be delivered from evil and the evil one. As you pray, remember, dear one, His is the kingdom and the power and the glory forever and ever and ever. We win because He has already won. He watched and prayed and said, "Not My will, but Yours be done" (Luke 22:42).

D on't you just love your relationship with the Father? I was
reminded again this week how powerful prayer can be when
it begins and ends with worship. I will miss our time together. But I
know that if you continue to discipline yourself to discover truth for
yourself and live in the light of it, God will bring you to even greater
maturity and usefulness in His kingdom.

Now, there are still two days to go and *then* we will have completed our four weeks, or 28 days, of study. May I suggest that on
Saturday you review the first two weeks of study and focus your
prayers on the portion of the Lord's Prayer covered within that
framework of time. As you do, think about the way your prayer life
has changed during these last 26 days. Have you felt more fulfilled?
What has happened? It would be good to write it out below so you
can come back and read it later.

_____

_____

_____

_____

_____

_____

On Sunday, review the last two weeks of your study and then
ask the Lord to direct you to another person—or persons—with
whom you can share what you learned, even as Jesus shared with
His disciples.

Do you realize, Beloved, how many people there are who can
recite the Lord's Prayer but who don't realize what they are reciting,

who don't know this is a *way to pray*? A way to pray that can open a whole new realm of prayer! Have you thought of the ministry you could have in leading a study of this book in your home, your neighborhood, a nursing home, a Sunday school class? So often there is a ministry waiting for us...an answer to the prayer of some individual who is crying out for help, longing to know what to do, longing to know God and His Word more intimately.

You, beloved of God, could be their answer to prayer.

Questions for Group Discussion

Notes

Week One

Discuss Acts 6:2-4. Why did "the twelve" do this? What was their purpose?

Compare John 17:17 and John 15:7. Why is the Word so necessary? How can you ask and receive what you have asked for? How are the Word and asking connected?

If you are in the midst of the busyness of the day or even an overwhelming crisis, how can you apply these principles to your life?

What does it mean to "pray without ceasing"? Why would you need to pray without ceasing?

When the disciples asked Jesus to teach them to pray, how did He respond?

Discuss what you learned in general about prayer from Matthew 6:6-13.

As you discuss the first index sentence, you might ask...

- How is it possible to address God as your Father? (See John 1:12-13; 1 Corinthians 15:1-8; Ephesians 1:13-14.)
- Have you believed in the Lord Jesus Christ? How do you know?
- How important is faith to prayer? (See Hebrews 11:1,6.)

- What does it mean to "hallow" God's name? What does God's name represent?
- Is it possible to take His name in vain? How?

Discuss the prayers in Day Five:
- How do these prayers begin?
- How is God worshipped? What is said about Him?
- How can you apply these truths in your prayer life?

How were you encouraged in this week's study?

Week Two

You might find it helpful to say the Lord's Prayer together and review the topics of each sentence.

Discuss what you learned about God in the prayers of Hannah, Jeremiah, and Daniel. What do they say about God?

What is the topic of the second index sentence in the Lord's Prayer?

What does it mean to say, "Your kingdom come"?

Use the questions in Day Seven to help discuss Matthew 28:18-20:
- How does this passage relate to the second topic?
- What seems to be the priorities of those around you? Why do you think that is so?
- What do you need to do?

Discuss what you learned about our adversary in Matthew 4:8-10:

- What was the devil offering Jesus? Could he tempt a believer the same way?
- How does Jesus answer Satan? Should we do the same?

Are *worship* and *allegiance* synonymous? Give reasons for your answer.

What kind of allegiance does God expect?

What did you learn about the gospel of the kingdom in Matthew 24:14 and Revelation 14:6-7? What does this tell you about the heart of God?

How might this relate to Matthew 28:19-20?

What does it mean to say, "Your will be done, on earth as it is in heaven"?

Is there a relationship between submission and salvation? Use some of the questions in Day Nine (Matthew 7:21-27) to help with this discussion.

What did you learn from Jesus' example of prayer in the garden of Gethsemane?

How is the work of the kingdom accomplished?

How can you be filled with the knowledge of God's will? Would there be evidence of that knowledge of His will? Would your allegiance be shown?

Week Three

How do index sentences help us pray? Review the topics of the index sentences.

What is the change that occurs between verses 10 and 11?

Ask the questions on Day Eleven that relate to Romans 12:1-2 (on page 101). How do these things relate to the first three topics of the Lord's Prayer?

How is intercession seen in the Lord's Prayer?

What is the picture of intercessory prayer given in Exodus 28? What did you learn about Jesus from Isaiah 53:12? For whom does He intercede?

Discuss what you learned about Jesus in the Hebrews passages:
- Who is Jesus?
- Who does He save forever?
- What does He do? When?

Do you know another child of God who interceded for you to be saved? Are you to do the same?

What is the Holy Spirit's role in intercessory prayer?

What do we learn about faith in Hebrews 11:1-3? How can we know that "the worlds were prepared by the word of God"? What does this understanding have to do with prayer?

What does praying, "Give us this day our daily bread," show about your relationship with God? Are you depending on Him to meet your needs today and tomorrow?

How important is asking? Why do you think God wants us to ask when He already knows our needs?

Discuss James 4:1-3.
- What is the conflict? Why?
- Why were they not receiving what they asked for?
- What does James say about the world?
- What is a person like who tries to meet his or her own needs?

How does the kind of "asking" the Lord Jesus taught stop worry? (See Matthew 6:31-34.) For what are we to ask?

What does it mean to "plead the promises of God"?

Discuss what was learned from the passages in Day Fifteen about asking:
- When does Jesus hear?
- What are the promises?
- Does this mean you can ask and have anything you want?

What does it mean to ask according to the will of God? Does knowing His Word help understand His will?

How often are you to "ask"? What did you learn from the parable in Luke 18?

What did you learn about God this week? How will this knowledge help you in prayer?

Week Four

Say the Lord's Prayer together and review the topics.

Why are sin and forgiveness not dealt with immediately in this prayer?

How do transgressions against others compare to your transgressions against a Holy God?

What did you learn from Hebrews 12:9-11 about discipline? For whom is this discipline? Why? What are the results?

Why do we need to confess sin again? How do the Scripture passages in Day Sixteen help answer this question?

Talk about 1 John 1:9:

- Is this an encouragement to you?
- If there is no conviction of sin is there salvation?

How does Matthew 6:14-15 compare with Ephesians 4:31-32? Why is forgiveness necessary?

What is to be forgiven, according to Colossians 3:12-13? How often must I forgive? (See Matthew 18:21-25.) Are you withholding forgiveness?

What is revival? Where is it seen? What happens when sin is ignored? Why is sin likened to leaven?

Is your heart broken over the things that break God's heart? Why or why not? Do you sigh and groan over sin in your society?

What did you learn about sin in Daniel 9:1-22, Ezra 9:1-10, or both? What was the result of intercession?

What is the sixth index sentence dealing with? Does God tempt us to sin? How do you know?

What is to be your response in a trial? How important is having the Scripture hidden in your heart at that moment of temptation?

Discuss Matthew 26:36-46, using the questions in Day Nineteen to discuss this passage (on page 166).

If time allows, let someone from your group share how the Lord has delivered him or her in time of temptation.

What did you learn about prayer and deliverance from the passages in Day Twenty? Will God still deliver us like this today?

How vital is your role in praying for other believers around the world?

What is the topic of the seventh index sentence? Why?

Has this study changed your prayer time? How? Will you share these truths with others so their prayer life can be changed as well?

Notes

1. This is probably the most popular book I have written. It's been translated into many languages. It has accompanying CDs and DVDs (you can see what I looked like when I was much younger!). If you want more information on this study or the accompanying children's study, go to **www.precept.org**, call **1-800-763-8280**, or write **Precept Ministries International, PO Box 182218, Chattanooga, TN 37422.**

2. "The Sermons of John Wesley," 2006, http://new.gbgm-umc.org/umhistory/wesley/sermons/26/ (viewed December 7, 2006).

3. I just want you to remember that "hating" is simply used as a term of comparison. We are not to hate, but to love. We are to honor our parents—it is one of the commandments. Keep in mind that God never contradicts His Word—therefore this is saying that all other relationships in comparison to our love to Him must seem like "hatred." God is to be supremely loved and obeyed; which of course is only right, because He is God!

4. Basil Miller, *George Muller: Man of Faith and Miracles* (Minneapolis, MN: Bethany House Publishers, 1941), pp. 50-51.

5. Miller, pp. 50-51.

6. Robert J. Morgan, *On This Day* (Nashville, TN: Thomas Nelson Publishers, 1997), January 15. Used by permission.

7. "Christmas Eve in Romania," *A Bible for Russia* newsletter, December 1983. The author and publisher were unable to locate the copyright holder of this material, but will be pleased to make any necessary corrections in future editions.

8. Armin Gesswein's School of Prayer, "Plead the Promises of God!" pamphlet (Pasadena, CA: International Intercessors, n.d.). The author and publisher were unable to locate the copyright holder of this material, but will be pleased to make any necessary corrections in future editions.

9. Unidentified letter from a Precept leader. The author and publisher were unable to locate the copyright holder of this material, but will be pleased to make any necessary corrections in future editions.

10. If you are not familiar with what God's Word teaches on the subject of spiritual warfare, may I recommend my 11-week study *Lord, Is It Warfare? Teach Me to Stand.* It is a book that has been mightily used of God to help people win the battle skirmish by skirmish, as it teaches everything the Bible has to say on the subject of spiritual warfare. Teaching CDs and DVDs are also available.

Books in the
New Inductive Study Series

HARVEST HOUSE BOOKS BY KAY ARTHUR

ᖚᖚᖚᖚ

Discover the Bible for Yourself
God, Are You There?
God, Help Me Experience More of You
God, How Can I Live?
Lord, Help Me Grow Spiritually Strong in 28 Days
How to Study Your Bible
Israel, My Beloved
Just a Moment with You, God
Lord, Teach Me to Pray in 28 Days
Lord, Teach Me to Study the Bible in 28 Days
A Marriage Without Regrets
A Marriage Without Regrets Study Guide
Powerful Moments with God
Speak to My Heart, God
With an Everlasting Love
Youniquely Woman (with Emilie Barnes and Donna Otto)

ᖚᖚᖚ

Bibles
The New Inductive Study Bible (NASB)

ᖚᖚᖚ

Discover 4 Yourself® Inductive Bible Studies for Kids

God, What's Your Name?
How to Study Your Bible for Kids
Lord, Teach Me to Pray for Kids
God's Amazing Creation (Genesis 1–2)
Digging Up the Past (Genesis 3–11)
Abraham—God's Brave Explorer (Genesis 11–25)
Extreme Adventures with God (Isaac, Esau, and Jacob)
Joseph—God's Superhero (Genesis 37–50)
You're a Brave Man, Daniel! (Daniel 1–6)
Fast-Forward to the Future (Daniel 7–12)
Wrong Way, Jonah! (Jonah)
Jesus in the Spotlight (John 1–11)
Jesus—Awesome Power, Awesome Love (John 11–16)
Jesus—To Eternity and Beyond! (John 17–21)
Becoming God's Champion (2 Timothy)
Boy, Have I Got Problems! (James)
Bible Prophecy for Kids (Revelation 1–7)
A Sneak Peek into the Future (Revelation 8–22)

NEW AMERICAN STANDARD BIBLE
UPDATED EDITION

THE NEW
INDUCTIVE
STUDY BIBLE

DISCOVERING THE TRUTH FOR YOURSELF

CHANGING THE WAY
PEOPLE STUDY GOD'S WORD

"Inductive study of the Bible is the best way to discover scriptural truth... There is no jewel more precious than that which you have mined yourself."

—HOWARD HENDRICKS

Every feature is designed to help you gain a more intimate understanding of God and His Word. This study Bible, the only one based entirely on the inductive study approach, provides you with the tools for observing what the text says, interpreting what it means, and applying it to your life.